Penguin Handbooks

# THE YOGHURT BOOK

Arto der Haroutunian was born in Aleppo, Syria, where his family had settled, but was educated in Britain, where he qualified as an architect and set up his own practice.

With his brother he opened their first Armenian restaurant in 1969 when his interest in food in general and Middle Eastern food in particular really commenced. He has written extensively on the subject.

Outside his architect and restaurateur roles he is better known as a painter and he has had several major exhibitions. He is married, with a young son.

# CONTENTS

# INTRODUCTION

*I owe my health and age to yoghurt, nothing else – not even God!*
M. Husseynov at the age of 147

When my family emigrated to Britain about thirty years ago with all our domestic paraphernalia including pots and pans, thick woollen blankets, a large packet of Turkish coffee, some dried aubergines, courgettes and okra – vegetables unheard of by the British public in those days – as well as old personal relics, my mother brought with her in her handbag a small jar of yoghurt which, she proudly announced, was to be the 'starter' for the new bowl of yoghurt she intended to make on our arrival. The starter of that same jar had been brought over from the 'old country' – Armenia, where my family originated – years before and, no doubt in some form or other, had been in our family for generations. Talk about eternity! Indeed, what I really should have said at the start is that yoghurt begets yoghurt; it is eternal. Let me explain.

The Russian-born French bacteriologist Dr Illya Metchnikoff (1845 –1916), director of the Pasteur Institute in Paris and, in 1908, co-winner of the Nobel Prize for physiology and medicine (for his work on the infection-fighting properties of white blood cells) carried out a great deal of his research in the Balkans amongst the Bulgarian peasantry who, though extremely impoverished, had an average life expectancy of eighty-seven years. He concluded that this remarkable longevity was partly due to a drink called yoghurt. In his laboratory he isolated the two types of bacilli (*Lactobacillus bulgaricus* and *Streptococcus thermophilus*) that are responsible for changing milk to yoghurt. Metchnikoff proved scientifically what Middle Eastern people had known for centuries, that yoghurt – a fermented, slightly acid, semi-solid cultured milk related to other fermented milks – arrested

7

internal putrefaction, has antibiotic properties which restore normal intestinal equilibrium and is excellent for the aged, the young and people with a weak digestion. Yoghurt contains a higher percentage of lactic acid, $C_3H_6O_3$, the acid formed in milk, than other fermented milks and is very rich in vitamin $B_2$ complex. It has no more calories than milk. The yoghurt culture remains alive even after the passage through the intestine whereas the bacillus of other milk products is destroyed.

In the Caucasus, people have believed in the healing power of yoghurt for centuries. They have attributed their longevity to it and have maintained, for example, that yoghurt with garlic is an excellent cure for tuberculosis, that it helps dysentery, averts a hangover, increases sexual potency and even remedies baldness!

I remember that as a child I came to detest that thick, white, jelly-like food simply because I was forced to eat it day in, day out, on its own, with honey, as a salad or a drink, in stews or soups. Now, however, with the accumulation of grey hair and creeping middle age I have come to see not only its many benefits but I have come to like it so much that, like a born-again believer, I have compiled this book of recipes to demonstrate how versatile and exciting yoghurt can be.

The name 'yoghurt' is said to be either Bulgarian or Turkish in origin. This is not so. It is Armenian and derives from two Indo-European roots – *yough* (oil) and *gurd* (curd; *guard* in Armenian). Thus *yough-guard* means the oil of the curd, i.e. the whey. *Masta* on the other hand means curdled milk in Sanskrit. This has been passed into Persian and Kurdish as *mast* and into Armenian as *madz-oon*. In Armenian *ma-guard* is the bacillus, i.e. the curd of the *masta*. Thus today, when we say 'yoghurt' what we really mean is the whey and not the curd. For the sake of accuracy we should call it either *masta* or *mast* or *madzoon*. We must also remember that while the above languages are Indo-European and the people Indo-Aryan by origin, both the Bulgarian and Turkish people, in language and origin, are of Mongolian stock, with a language that belongs to the Altaic family.

There are many fanciful and semi-mythological stories on the origin of yoghurt. Here are a few for interest.

The Tajik and Mongolian nomadic tribes carried their milk in gourds strung over the backs of camels. Sunshine and the constant jolting turned it thick and sour.

Early Greeks and desert nomads used to have their goats' and sheep's milk exposed to the bacteria of the open air and thus it developed a new character.

Finally, the best of all, when Noah's Ark was floating over the waves and the animals produced all that milk poor old Noah had nowhere to store it and so he used sewn-up bags made of animal stomachs and, to his great surprise, one day he found that the milk had thickened. At first he must have thought 'what a waste', but when he tried it he liked the flavour and thus yoghurt was born. However fanciful this last explanation is, it is very probably nearest to the truth, for the lining of a calf's stomach contains an enzyme, rennin, which produces rennet – the curdling agent.

Round about 10,000 BC the Aryan tribes made their appearance in eastern Turkey, northern Iran and the north-west of India. They left a great religious compendium known as the 'Vedas', the most important of which is the *Rig Veda*, written over three thousand years ago. It reflects the religious beliefs, the customs and thoughts of the people who wrote it. Agriculture was the main activity of the Aryans. They tilled the soil with ploughs pulled by oxen – a custom that still persists in Turkey, Iran and India. The Aryans' herds were one of their main sources of wealth. The cow, which provided milk, was held in great esteem – as it still is in India. Milk and butter were the staple foods of the Aryans and were offered as libations to the gods. The Aryans also ate flesh. They were great hunters, killing their game with bows and arrows or using ingenious traps. They grilled the meat on open fires.

Agri was the god of fire, and he engendered the other gods. *Soma* or *homa* – the ambrosia of other races – was the fermented liquid which gave force to Agri, made the gods immortal and filled men with vigour. I believe this was none other than *masta* (yoghurt), to which was added the plant *homa* (*Sarcostema vininelis*). The result, a strong, intoxicating brew, which was considered healthy, nutritious and capable of providing strength as well as prolonging life, was truly the food of the gods! Indeed, amongst the Yogis, yoghurt mixed with honey is still considered a food of the gods and the name of the ancient Zoroastrian supreme deity 'Ahura-Masta' ('Ara-mast' in Armenian), meaning 'all-powerful Masta', clearly reflects the great importance the Aryan tribes attributed to curdled milk.

There is no doubt that yoghurt and yoghurt-based dishes have played an important role in the diet of the Aryan races. However it did not remain their prerogative for long; its existence and uses were, in time, passed on to other people. References to yoghurt and other curdled milks abound in the written records of ancient civilizations. The Egyptians and Israelites favoured it. The Greeks were aware of its healthful properties and the historians Herodotus and Pliny the Elder wrote about cultured milks.

Throughout the ages conquering races – Arabs and then Turks – helped to spread yoghurt from its 'homeland' (i.e. the area of the Middle East which today comprises the states of Turkey, Armenia, Kurdistan and most of Iran) to the neighbouring lands as far as Romania in the west and India in the east. From the Aryan Persians the Arabians acquired the knowledge of rice, tea and yoghurt, which they called *Halib-el-Ajam* (Persian milk). The Persians also spread its popularity throughout Afghanistan, northern India and Pakistan. Interestingly enough there is no yoghurt today in China, Japan, Korea, Mongolia and even in most of central Asia. Yoghurt is known in northern Egypt, but is not popular. It is little used in the north African cuisine and the yoghurt eaten in Ethiopia, Sudan and Somalia is more of a curdled milk than a true yoghurt.

There has for centuries been controversy in the Middle East between peoples – especially Greeks and Turks – about the origin of certain dishes. One claims all is really his, the other screams '*Yok*' – No! As with everything in life, nothing belongs to one man. Food varies, it is developed and adapted in response to economic and cultural pressure. All that man has created or, should I say, adapted from nature is man's. The name may change, he may favour one or other ingredient, but in essence the product is the same – nature's.

For centuries the people of the Middle East, by whatever name they are known, have used yoghurt. Today it has broken through to the West, has gained respectability and become one of the 'in' things; worshipped by the nature–food lovers, clinically approved by the scientists and tolerated by the *haute cuisine* priests. The introduction of yoghurt into western Europe is attributed to the French king François I, after he had been cured by an Armenian healer from Constantinople who, arriving on foot with a herd of goats, prepared (in great secrecy) a batch of yoghurt and prescribed it to the monarch, restored his health and returned home – presumably still on foot! Despite a few pockets of devotees (Armenian, Jewish, and Greek merchants) and some flurries of interest down through the centuries, nobody in the West even knew or cared about yoghurt – until Metchnikoff. After his death a Spaniard named Issac Carasso opened the first modern yoghurt plants in Barcelona and Paris. During and after the Second World War the Carasso family business opened other factories in the USA and France, marketing their product under the brand name of 'Dannon' ('Danone' in France). The first commercially produced yoghurt in the USA was sold under the name of 'Madzoon' in the early 1920s. In 1929 the Colombosian family introduced a whole-milk yoghurt, 'Colombo', which is still highly popular on the east coast of the USA, while the Kazanis family sold their produce under the label of 'Oxyzala'. In Britain in the early 1930s 'Yegvart's Yogurt' was highly popular in the north-west.

These early pioneering families were Middle Easterners and, indeed, it could not have been otherwise for, just as with my own mother, many other Middle Eastern women brought over with them to the West a jar or two of the 'food of the gods' as an inherent part of their culture and traditions. Indeed the first reported appearance of yoghurt in the Americas was 1784 when Armenian and Greek immigrants, fleeing the harsh Ottoman misrule, brought with them the dried yoghurt culture and prepared their favourite food as they had back in the 'old country'.

Today in Britain, France and particularly the USA, yoghurt is big business, with several major concerns fighting for ever-increasing markets and offering the consumer a vast choice – natural yoghurt, fruit yoghurt, sweetened yoghurt and frozen yoghurt. It was decided by early manufacturers that yoghurt should be given a new look. Therefore the first step was to prepare it with partially skimmed milk thus reducing the calorie content without affecting the nutritive value. In contrast the Middle Eastern and most home-made versions tend to be very rich and creamy with a tart flavour as they are made with whole milk. The next step was to remove the tart flavour of plain yoghurt by sweetening it. This was done by adding fruit preserves and flavours. Indeed, the sweetening of yoghurt was the prime reason for its sudden popularity throughout the West, where it is still consumed primarily as a snack or dessert.

But yoghurt is more than a dessert. Its versatility has been known for centuries by the people of the Middle East, Caucasus, the Balkans and India where it appears in soups, salads, sauces, stews, pastries and sweets, enhancing and enriching the food, giving it flavour and a touch of magic. In the West most people do not know of the many uses of yoghurt, hence this book, which I hope will be the 'starter' for your experiments with this many-faceted ingredient worthy of the gods! With yoghurt almost anything goes. The possibilities of cooking with it are infinite. It is a good substitute for cream, milk, buttermilk and soured cream. It makes an excellent marinade, and goes well with vegetables, eggs, meat, poultry, cheese and grains.

In this book I have collected recipes from all over the lands where yoghurt has always been used. Most are very old, some relatively new and a few are adaptations of old recipes where I suggest yoghurt was once used – or should have been. My sources are varied – ancient manuscripts, old cookery books, a poem or two, friends, relations, relations of friends and friends of relations. I have found one book on yoghurt by Irfan Orga, *Cooking with Yogurt* (Andre Deutsch, 1956), which I have consulted with pleasure. Some of the recipes have been eye-openers to me and I have included a few in my collection.

My advice is first to use these recipes and then to make up your own, thus enriching not only your taste and palate, but the use of yoghurt.

I believe that of all the Middle Eastern ingredients and forms of cooking, yoghurt is by far the most exciting, not only in what it already offers, but because in Europe and America where it is very new countless variations and new uses will be found in the years to come.

## Quantities

All the recipes are for four people, unless otherwise indicated.

## Metrication

I have not always used exact equivalents for quantities in the metric and imperial systems. I have tried to make the measurements in both systems easily workable, while keeping the proportions right. It is therefore important when using the recipes to stick to either imperial or metric measurements – do not mix them.

## Spoons

Where quantities are measured in teaspoons or tablespoons use a *level* spoonful. One teaspoon = 5ml; 1 tablespoon = 15ml.

## Glossary

There is a glossary of the less familiar ingredients on pp. 197–8.

# HOW TO MAKE YOGHURT;
# BASIC YOGHURT RECIPES
## BASIC DATA

### Bacteria

Yoghurt is made with a culture containing beneficial bacteria (*Lactobacillus bulgaricus* and *Streptococcus thermophilus*) which are allowed to multiply freely in milk at a controlled temperature until it achieves the proper semi-solid consistency and tart flavour. The bacteria are rich in vitamin B – excellent for maintaining a healthy intestinal system.

### Contents

8 fl oz (225ml) of plain yoghurt made from partially skimmed milk contains:

> 89 per cent water
> 125 calories (150 if made with whole milk, more if flavourings are added)
> 8g protein
> 4g fat
> 13g carbohydrate
> 294mg calcium
> 1mg iron
> 170 units vitamin A
> 10mg thiamine
> 44mg riboflavin
> 2mg niacin
> 2mg ascorbic acid

Yoghurt is a particularly good source of calcium.

## Freezing

Do not freeze as freezing and thawing adversely affect the smooth texture.

## Refrigeration

Yoghurt prepared in the home should be refrigerated in order to halt any further growth of bacteria. It will then keep for up to a week before it starts to become too acid. Commercial yoghurt should be refrigerated immediately after purchase and should be consumed within three to four days – otherwise the acidity will continue to increase and so a sharper flavour will be produced.

## Whey

This is the watery part of the milk which separates from the curds after coagulation. This is the real yoghurt (see p. 8). It is used extensively in Iranian and Indian cuisine.

### YOGHURT MAKES YOGHURT

Just a little yoghurt – about one teaspoon to a pint (½l) of milk– when put into warm milk will make more yoghurt. How? because it is its own 'bacillus' or starter.

Any commercial natural yoghurt can be used as a starter and thereafter your own yoghurt will supply the bacillus needed. There are several methods of yoghurt preparation. Here is the simple, age-old method handed down from generation to generation – in my opinion, the best.

*2 pints (1 litre) milk*
*1 tablespoon yoghurt – or starter*

1 Bring the milk to the boil in a saucepan.
2 When the froth rises turn off the heat.
3 Allow the milk to cool to the point where you can dip your finger

in and count up to fifteen – without screaming! This is to ascertain that the correct temperature has been reached. As we are dealing with living bacteria it is essential that the temperature is kept between 120°F (49°C), above which it will be killed, and 90°F (32°C), below which it will not grow.

4 Remove the skin that has formed on the surface of the milk. (This is the cream. Let it cool, add some sugar to it and eat it spread on a piece of bread. I rate this as one of the great luxuries of life! This cream is called *ser* or *kaymak* and is highly prized throughout the Middle East, where it is made very thick and is consumed for breakfast. It is also a basic ingredient of many desserts.)

5 Beat the yoghurt (starter) in a cup, add a tablespoon of the warm milk, beat vigorously and pour into the rest of the milk.

6 Empty the milk into an earthenware or glass bowl and stir a few times.

7 Cover the bowl with a large plate and wrap in a towel or tea-towel.

8 Put in a warm place (e.g. in an airing cupboard or near a radiator or fireplace) and do not disturb for 8 to 10 hours.

Yoghurt can be kept for up to a week in the fridge. When it is nearly finished make a new batch by using a little starter from the previous batch.

Home-made yoghurt is not only cheaper than shop-bought, it is also much nicer because it is less acidic – yoghurt gets sourer with age – and is lighter in texture.

### The optimistic approach

This recipe reminds me of a would-be great entrepreneur who was seen seated at the seaside pouring yoghurt out from large cups into the water and then stirring it vigorously with a large wooden spoon.

A friend passed by and asked, 'What are you doing?'

'Making yoghurt.'

'You're joking. How can you make yoghurt? It is impossible, it couldn't possibly hold. I mean, it's water, not milk!'

'Yes, I agree the chances of it working are very slim, but just visualize if it does . . . I mean, just think of the fortune to be made.'

The friend is stunned, amazed, mesmerized.

'Here, let me give you a hand.'

'No thanks, I'll tell you what you can do.'

'What?'

'Go and buy a ton of cucumber and we'll have a sea full of *jajig*.'

'A wonderful idea.' The friend rushes off to the market.

'Don't bother with the salt,' the entrepreneur shouts after him, 'it's already salted.'

### Alternative methods of making yoghurt

There are many different kinds of yoghurt-making equipment available today. They all work well. Some electric yoghurt makers are fairly expensive, but they make the process completely effortless, as you need not heat the milk or use a thermometer. The machine does all the work.

Another method involves using an insulated jar – an Insulex or thermos flask. This method makes good yoghurt but has one drawback: after the setting time you should decant the yoghurt into a bowl to chill for otherwise it over-incubates and becomes too acidic. Personally I prefer to stick to the tried and true method. Use a thermometer if you do not trust your finger.

### A few further hints

1  Use absolutely clean, well-rinsed utensils and containers.

2  If you use sterilized milk rather than pasteurized it is not necessary to bring it to the boil first. Simply heat it to the required temperature (110°F, 43°C).

3  If you are slimming use liquid skimmed milk instead of whole milk.

4  If there is no yoghurt starter or bacillus available you can use dried powder culture which can be bought from health shops or some large chemists.

5  If you want a thicker, creamier yoghurt stir skimmed milk powder into the milk at the outset – 1 tablespoon to each pint (½l) milk.

### Regulating the taste

The taste of home-made yoghurt can be regulated. For a mild flavour chill as soon as the yoghurt begins to thicken. For a stronger flavour incubate it for a longer period.

### Reasons for failure

You may find that occasionally your yoghurt will not set and will separate instead into curds and whey. The main causes of this are:

1  The milk was not at the right temperature, i.e. between 90°F (32°C) and 120°F (49°C), when the starter was added.

2  The incubation temperature was either too low or too high.

3  The wrong amount of starter was added. Either too much or too little will cause it to separate.

### Flavours

If you wish to flavour your yoghurt then it is best to do so after it has thickened. It is much easier to achieve the actual taste you require and it prevents the flavourings from sinking, which they tend to do – especially if you are using pieces of fruit.

### Stabilizing yoghurt

If you are going to use yoghurt in a recipe which involves boiling the yoghurt it is necessary to stabilize it first or it will separate and appear lumpy. This will not actually affect the taste, but will simply make the dish a little less attractive. If you cannot eat all the fresh yoghurt you have before it becomes too acid, then stabilize it and use it for cooking.

To stabilize the yoghurt *either* stir 1 dessertspoon flour into a little water and then add to the yoghurt before cooking, *or* beat an egg into the yoghurt before cooking. Note that once yoghurt has been stabilized and boiled it cannot be used as a starter, as the bacteria die at high temperatures.

## LABNA
### *Cream cheese*

This appetizer is a must on any Syrian or Lebanese breakfast table, where it is consumed with hot pitta bread.

1 Make the yoghurt (see p. 14). I suggest you try making *labna* with a pint (½l) of yoghurt first. You can increase the quantity later if you find that you like it and are going to consume it in vast quantities!

2 *Either* line a colander with a piece of damp muslin, *or* sew a muslin or loosely woven cotton bag with a drawstring top about 12 × 12 ins (30 × 30cm) in size.

3 Spoon the yoghurt into the colander or bag and leave to drain for 5 to 6 hours in the sink (or suspend the bag over a bowl). The whey will drain away leaving a light, soft, creamy cheese.

4 Serve it on a small plate, sprinkled with a little dried mint or some other herb (chopped dill, parsley, chives, tarragon) or with a little olive oil poured over the top.

5 Decorate with a pinch of paprika and a few black olives. Serve it for breakfast or as an hors d'oeuvre.

## MADZNA BANIR
### *Yoghurt cheese*

A charming and simple Armenian hors d'oeuvre. *Labna* (see previous recipe) is shaped into small balls, drenched in olive oil and then sprinkled with fresh herbs. Serve as an appetizer with *lavash* or pitta bread and a glass of arak (or any favourite aperitif).

*1½ pints (1l) yoghurt*
*1 teaspoon salt*
*about 3 fl oz (100ml) olive oil*
*1 tablespoon chopped fresh mint*
*1 tablespoon chopped fresh dill*

*2 tablespoons finely chopped spring onions*
*1 tablespoon finely chopped fresh chives*

1 Mix the yoghurt and salt and drain as for *labna*, above.

2 Spoon the thickened yoghurt into a bowl and then shape into walnut-sized balls.

**3** Arrange the balls on a large serving plate and pour the olive oil over them.

**4** Mix all the herbs together in a bowl and then sprinkle them over the balls.


## DAHI, URGO

*Dahi* is the Indian name for yoghurt and *urgo* is the Ethiopian. Both are names for the same thing, but it is not yoghurt as we know it. It is, in reality, milk curdled with the addition of a few drops of lemon juice and stirred continuously until the milk has completely curdled. The milk is covered and left for 15 to 20 minutes and then the curds are strained from the whey. (Turkish peasants sometimes squeeze in a few drops of fresh fig juice to curdle the milk.)

The Ethiopians and other neighbouring nationalities consume a great deal of *urgo*. Since their diet consists basically of a sour spongy bread called *unjara* – made of *fef* (wheat) – and generally hot and spicy food, *urgo* is the ideal accompaniment. It is almost always served with meals both at home and in restaurants.

It will not act as a bacillus or starter, but it makes excellent curd cheese.


## PANIR
### Indian cream cheese

*Panir* in Hindi, *panir* and *banir* in Iranian and Armenian and *beynir* in Turkish all refer to the same thing – cream cheese made from milk. It is extensively used in both savoury and sweet dishes and is a less sophisticated form of *labna* or *chortan*. It is used in such dishes as *matar panir* (peas with fresh cheese – see p. 85) and many other vegetable dishes where, as well as adding extra nutrition, it helps balance the strong, spicy flavours of most Indian dishes. There is a recipe for *ras gula* (*panir* in syrup) in the section dealing with sweets (p. 185).

*2½ pints (1½l) milk*
*1 tablespoon lemon juice*

**1** Bring the milk to the boil in a saucepan, stirring from time to time to prevent a skin forming.

**2** Remove from the heat and gradually add the lemon juice, stirring continuously until the milk has curdled completely.

**3** Cover and leave for 15 to 20 minutes.

**4** Strain through a muslin cloth to ensure that all the watery whey is removed.

**5** Wrap the loose curds – *chenna* in Hindi – and compress with a weight for 2 to 3 hours.

**6** The cheese can then be stored in the refrigerator and cut into cubes whenever needed.

## CHORTAN
### *Dried yoghurt balls*

In ancient times, and in some villages even today, Armenian women used to make yoghurt, then drain it as with *labna*, dry it in the sun and then store it to use at any time of the year in soups.

**1** Prepare the *labna* (see p. 18).

**2** Knead it well.

**3** Make it into walnut sized balls.

**4** Arrange the balls on a tray and dry. As there is little sun to speak of in many European countries I suggest that the balls are placed on a tray and kept in a dry place for about 48 hours and then perhaps left in the oven at the lowest temperature for 24 hours. The result is not the same as sun-dried *chortan* but it is the nearest substitute.

**5** When the *chortan* balls are thoroughly dry they should be as hard as stone.

**6** Store them in an airtight jar and use as required.

When using *chortan* balls to make yoghurt soups (*spas* or *madzoona-bour*, see pp. 34 and 30), break two *chorton* balls with a sharp knife. The yoghurt will have become powdery and should dissolve easily in water. Add the water – 2 pints (1l) to every two *chorton* balls – and stir well to dissolve. You can then use this liquid to prepare whichever type of yoghurt soup you require (see next chapter).

## SURKI
### *Spiced dried yoghurt*

These are apple-sized balls of dried, spiced yoghurt covered in thyme leaves, which are kept in airtight jars for months. They are excellent in salads such as *surki aghtsan* (p. 72). They are also sometimes stored in olive oil. This keeps them soft and they are then used to make *zeytov surki* (p. 73).

*Surki*, the pride of Cilician Armenians, is known as *chaklish* by the Arabs of the region and as *chokeleg* by the local Assyrians and Turks.

Instead of yoghurt, you can use cottage cheese, which is an excellent substitute for the *labna* made from milk.

The quantities given will make four fair-sized *surki* balls.

Labna *made from 4 pints (2l)*
   *yoghurt or 2 lb (1kg) cottage*
   *cheese*
2 *teaspoons oregano*
1 *teaspoon ground cumin*

1 *teaspoon allspice*
½ *teaspoon chilli powder*
4 *oz (100g) fresh thyme leaves,*
   *coarsely chopped*

1 Empty the *labna* into a bowl, knead it well and mix in the oregano, cumin, allspice and chilli pepper. If you are using cottage cheese, then mix and add the spices as with the *labna*, and blend in a liquidizer to get the same smooth effect.

2 Divide the mixture into four and form balls.

3 Put on a tray and dry in the sun, or, as with *chortan*, keep in a warm place until the *surki* balls are fairly dry.

4 Cover the *surki* balls completely with the thyme leaves and keep in a warm place for 24 hours.

# SOUPS

First of all I must say that I find yoghurt an excellent ingredient for soup, perhaps because I was brought up on bowls of yoghurt soup of one kind or another. I am well aware that there are many other exciting soups – soups made with vegetables, with meat, grains, fruit, even flowers, and of course clear consommés, so popular in the European cuisine – but on a winter's night when the wind is howling outside, and the rain is splashing against the window panes, there is nothing better, I believe; than a bowl of hot yoghurt soup to ease, warm and satisfy one.

In the Orient, especially the Middle East, soups are often eaten as a meal in themselves, accompanied by thick brown bread or thin flat *lavash*. Yoghurt soups play a unique role in the cuisine of the Middle East. They do not so far exist in any other cuisine, surprisingly enough, not even in that of the Indian subcontinent, which indeed possesses very few soups of any kind in its repertoire. Naturally it is unheard of in the Far East, Africa – with the exception of Egypt, Libya and parts of Ethiopia – and the Americas.

Of all the Middle Eastern people I believe it is the Armenians and Iranians who have used yoghurt most, and yoghurt soup particularly: the former seem to prefer a simple treatment, in such favourites as *spas* and *madzoonabour* – a clear soup of yoghurt, chopped onions and dried mint; the latter revel in rich, almost lavishly ornamental, treatments as in *ash-e-jo*.

The possibilities for using yoghurt in soups are limitless. It is an excellent substitute for the soured cream popular throughout eastern Europe and the Balkans. It can often replace natural cream and mixes very well with most spices. There is nothing better on a hot summer's day than a bowl of cold yoghurt soup. Certain vegetables seem to have a great affinity with yoghurt – spinach, cucumber, onions, mint, rice and barley, for example. Vegetables such as aubergines, broccoli and mushrooms have not been much used with yoghurt but should be. I hope the few dishes that I have included in this selection suggest that the possibilities are rich. Indeed, anything goes with yoghurt – well almost – so the best way is to find out by experimenting.

## SUTERESI CHORBA
### *Watercress and yoghurt soup*

This is a Bulgarian soup also popular with Greeks and Turks. It is served chilled and is a delicious summer soup which also looks very attractive.

*3 bunches watercress*
*1½ pints (1l) chicken stock*
*2 oz (50g) walnuts*
*1 pint (600ml) yoghurt*
*1 teaspoon salt*
*½ teaspoon ground white pepper*

*2 tablespoons lemon juice*

GARNISH
*some watercress sprigs*
*¼ pint (150ml) yoghurt*

1 Wash the watercress; trim off the coarse stems and any yellow leaves.

2 Place the chicken stock in a saucepan, add the watercress, bring to the boil and then simmer for about 15 minutes.

3 Strain the mixture into a colander, reserving the stock.

4 Place the watercress and walnuts in a blender and liquidize.

5 Pour this mixture into a large bowl, add the stock and stir in the yoghurt.

6 Season with the salt, pepper and lemon juice and leave to chill for a few hours in the refrigerator.

7 Taste and adjust seasoning if necessary.

8 Serve in individual bowls with a tablespoon of yoghurt swirled into the centre of each bowl of soup and garnished with a sprig of watercress.

# AB DOUGH KHIAR BA GOOSHT-E-MORGH
## *Cold yoghurt soup with chicken*

From Iran, nice, substantial and different. A typical example of the cuisine of that land, making use of many ingredients. Although this is traditionally a soup it could be served as a salad, as it is thick with chopped vegetables and meat.

2 medium-sized cucumbers
1 pint (600ml) yoghurt
1 teaspoon dried tarragon
1 teaspoon thyme
2 leeks, washed and chopped
1 sprig fresh mint, chopped
1 tablespoon raisins
1 small onion, finely chopped

1 teaspoon salt
pinch of pepper
1 tablespoon walnuts, chopped
1 hard-boiled egg, thinly sliced
1 breast of chicken (boiled or grilled)
1 oz (25g) butter
1 tablespoon dried mint

1 Peel the cucumbers and chop them finely.
2 In a large bowl mix the yoghurt and cucumber together.
3 Add the tarragon, thyme, leeks, mint and raisins, and stir well.
4 Add the onion, salt, pepper, walnuts and egg.
5 Bone the chicken, cut into fine pieces and add to the soup. Mix well.
6 Melt the butter in a small saucepan, sauté the mint and pour over the soup.
7 Serve cold.

# TARATOR CHORBA
## *Bulgarian yoghurt soup*

Bulgaria is famed for its excellent yoghurt and cheeses. This refreshing soup is ideal on a hot summer's day. Similar soups are found throughout the Balkans as well as Turkey.

1 pint (600ml) yoghurt
½ pint (300ml) milk
2 tablespoons sunflower oil or vegetable oil
1 tablespoon white vinegar
1 tablespoon lemon juice

4 oz (100g) cooked meat, chopped finely
4 heaped tablespoons cooked spaghetti, cut into short lengths
1 onion, finely chopped

| | |
|---|---|
| 2 tomatoes, blanched, peeled and | GARNISH |
|    coarsely chopped | ice cubes |
| 1 teaspoon salt | 1 oz (25g) walnuts, very finely |
| ½ teaspoon white pepper |    chopped |

**1** Put the yoghurt, milk, oil, vinegar, and lemon juice into a large bowl and whisk them together until smooth.

**2** Stir in all the remaining ingredients and taste to adjust seasoning.

**3** Spoon the soup into individual bowls, add an ice cube to each bowl and then garnish with the chopped walnuts.

## BROCCOLI YOGHURT SOUP

A simple yet unusual soup. It can be served either hot or cold.

| | |
|---|---|
| 1 lb (½kg) frozen broccoli | ½ teaspoon black pepper |
|    (thawed) | ½ teaspoon dried basil |
| 1 clove garlic | ½ teaspoon cumin powder |
| 1 pint (600ml) chicken stock | ½ pint (300ml) yoghurt |
| ½ teaspoon cayenne pepper | 1 tablespoon flour if the soup is to be |
| 1 teaspoon salt |    served hot |

**1** In a pan cook the broccoli in a little boiling water for about 10 minutes, or until tender.

**2** Discard water and allow the broccoli to cool.

**3** Squeeze out excess water.

**4** Spoon the broccoli into a blender and add the garlic, chicken stock, cayenne, salt, black pepper, basil and cumin powder.

**5** Blend until smooth.

FOR CHILLED SOUP:

**6** Add the yoghurt to the blender and blend for 2 to 3 seconds.

**7** Empty the contents of the blender into a glass bowl and chill in the refrigerator for 2 to 4 hours.

FOR HOT SOUP:

**8** Follow steps 1–5.

**9** Pour into a large saucepan and bring to the boil.

**10** Stir 1 tablespoon of flour into the yoghurt.

**11** Lower the heat, add the yoghurt and stir well. Bring just to the boil and serve immediately.

## CHERKEZ CHORBASI
### *Circassian vegetable soup with yoghurt*

This is a Caucasian soup, popular with the Circassians, who are famed for their beautiful women and fierce dances. The soup itself is wholesome and tasty, some people may even call it beautiful too!

1 onion, peeled and sliced
1 carrot, peeled and sliced
4 oz (100g) green beans, trimmed
   and sliced
4 oz (100g) green peas, podded
1 tablespoon long-grained rice,
   washed
½ pint (300ml) tomato juice

1 pint (600ml) stock
½ teaspoon thyme
½ teaspoon paprika
1 teaspoon salt
½ teaspoon black pepper
2 bay leaves
¼ pint (150ml) yoghurt

1 Put all the ingredients except the yoghurt into a large saucepan. If you are using frozen peas and beans rather than fresh ones then add them half-way through the cooking time.

2 Bring to the boil and then simmer until the vegetables are well cooked.

3 Stir in the yoghurt, bring to just below boiling point and serve immediately.

## SOUPA YAOURTI
### *Yoghurt soup with tomato*

This rather simple soup from Greece has a little wine added to the centre of each bowl just before serving.

1 pint (600ml) yoghurt
6 oz (175g) rice, washed thoroughly
   and drained
2 oz (50g) butter
1 teaspoon salt

2 large fresh tomatoes, blanched and
   skinned
a little white wine
2 tablespoons finely chopped parsley

1 Drain the yoghurt through a fine piece of muslin for about an hour to remove the whey.

2 Bring 2½ pints (1½l) water to the boil in a large saucepan, add the rice, butter and salt, and bring back to the boil, stirring constantly.

3 Mash the tomatoes and add to the soup.

4 Lower the heat and simmer until the rice is tender.

5 Pour the yoghurt into a mixing bowl and beat in 3–4 tablespoons of the soup until smooth.

6 Remove the soup from the heat and then stir in the yoghurt mixture.

7 When well blended ladle into individual bowls, spoon a little wine into each and top with some chopped parsley.

## ESHKENEH SHIRAZI
### *Fenugreek yoghurt soup*

This classic Iranian soup is from the region of Shiraz, the heart of ancient Persia. Fenugreek, a popular spice known to the Romans as 'Greek hay', is the seed of a plant belonging to the pea family. It has a bitter flavour and is used extensively in Iran, Armenia and, particularly, the Gulf States. You can purchase it from Middle-Eastern and Indian groceries.

1½ oz (40g) butter
1 onion, finely chopped
3 tablespoons flour
1 teaspoon fenugreek (chaiman *in* Turkish *or* shanbalileb *in* Iranian)

2 oz (50g) walnuts, coarsely chopped
1 teaspoon salt
½ teaspoon black pepper
1 pint (600ml) yoghurt
2 tablespoons fresh parsley, chopped

1 In a large saucepan melt the butter and fry the onion until golden brown.

2 Add the flour and stir until well blended.

3 Add the fenugreek and walnuts, and slowly stir in 2 pints (1¼l) hot water.

4 Season with the salt and pepper.

5 Bring to the boil, then lower the heat and simmer for 20 minutes. By this time the soup will have thickened a little.

6 Empty the yoghurt into a bowl, add a few tablespoons of the soup to it and stir thoroughly.

7 Slowly pour the yoghurt mixture into the soup pan, stirring constantly.

8 Heat through but do not allow to boil.

**9** Serve immediately, garnished with freshly chopped parsley.

NOTE If you like the flavour of fenugreek double the amount specified.

## ARMYANSKY BORSHT
### *Armenian borsht*

This soup, one of the most popular in Russia, is of Armenian origin. It makes use of yoghurt instead of the Russian *smetana* (soured cream) which gives the soup a much simpler and lighter flavour. It is a rich soup, nevertheless. Serve it hot with *lavash* or *naan* bread.

*1 medium raw beetroot*
*2 oz (50g) butter*
*½ onion, finely chopped*
*1 medium carrot, scraped and chopped*
*1 stick celery, chopped*
*4 oz (100g) finely sliced cabbage*
*2 oz (50g) mushrooms, finely sliced*

*1 small turnip, peeled and finely chopped*
*2½–3 pints (1½–1¾l) beef or lamb stock*
*1 lemon*
*2 teaspoons salt*
*1 teaspoon black pepper*
*½ pint (300ml) yoghurt*

**1** Place the whole beetroot, washed but unpeeled, in a small saucepan, cover with water, bring to the boil and simmer until cooked – about 30 minutes.

**2** Melt the butter in a large saucepan over a moderate heat.

**3** Add the prepared vegetables and sauté for a few minutes.

**4** Add the stock and simmer until the vegetables are just tender.

**5** Peel the beetroot, chop it and add to the soup. In this way most of the red colour should be retained.

**6** Pierce holes in the lemon and drop it into the soup – this will give it extra tartness.

**7** Add the seasoning and simmer for a further 10 to 15 minutes.

**8** Taste and adjust seasoning if necessary.

**9** Remove the lemon and discard it.

**10** To serve, spoon the soup into individual bowls and place two tablespoons of yoghurt in the centre of each.

## MADZOONABOUR
### *Yoghurt and mint soup*

Armenian soups tend to be lighter and simpler than the Iranian ones. This is by far the most popular of all Middle Eastern soups and the most original in its simplicity. The centenarians of Kharapak in the Caucasus swear by this soup.

| | |
|---|---|
| *1 pint (600ml) yoghurt* | *1 small onion, finely chopped* |
| *1 egg* | *2 teaspoons mint, dried and crushed* |
| *1 teaspoon salt* | *2 thick slices bread cut into ½ inch* |
| *¾ teaspoon black pepper* | *   (1cm) cubes* |
| *2 oz (50g) butter* | *cooking oil* |

 1  Put the yoghurt into a saucepan.

 2  Break the egg into the yoghurt and mix well with a wooden spoon.

 3  Put on a low heat and stir continuously until the yoghurt is just beginning to boil.

 4  Add 1 pint (600ml) water, season with the salt and pepper and return to the low heat.

 5  Meanwhile in a small saucepan melt the butter, add the chopped onion and mint and cook slowly until the onion is soft but not brown.

 6  When ready pour into the soup.

 7  Bring to the boil and simmer very gently for a few minutes.

 8  Heat a little cooking oil in a small saucepan. When it is very hot add the cubes of bread and fry until golden brown. Remove from the fat and put into a bowl.

 9  To serve, put the soup into individual bowls and add the croûtons at the last moment – the quantity depending on taste and appetite.

## ISTAKOZ ÇORBASI
### *Lobster soup*

This recipe from Istanbul has French overtones – due probably to the many European hotels and restaurants in that cosmopolitan city.

| | |
|---|---|
| *1 oz (25g) butter* | *2 lb (1kg) tomatoes, blanched,* |
| *2 onions, finely chopped* | *   skinned and sliced* |

1 clove garlic, crushed
1 teaspoon thyme – fresh if available
½ teaspoon ground fennel
¼ teaspoon ground nutmeg
1 teaspoon salt

½ teaspoon black pepper
¼ pint (150ml) dry white wine
1 average-sized lobster (cooked)
2 pints (1¼l) fish stock
¼ pint (150ml) yoghurt

1  Melt the butter in a large saucepan and sauté the onions until they are soft and translucent.

2  Add the tomatoes, garlic, thyme, fennel, nutmeg, salt and pepper; cover and simmer very gently for about ½ hour.

3  Add the wine, raise the heat and boil for 3 to 4 minutes.

4  Cut the lobster flesh into small pieces and add half to the saucepan together with the fish stock.

5  Cook for a further 15 minutes; remove from the heat.

6  Either put the soup through a sieve or whisk it in a blender until it is smooth.

7  Return to the saucepan, add the remaining pieces of lobster flesh and heat through.

8  Put the yoghurt in a small bowl, add a few tablespoons of the soup and beat with a wooden spoon until smooth.

9  Remove the soup from the heat, stir in the yoghurt and serve immediately.

## HAVABOUR
### Chicken with yoghurt soup

Armenian cuisine is rich in yoghurt-based dishes. This is a typical recipe from that land. Compare this chicken soup with that from Iran (p. 25) to see the difference in approach and treatment.

Serve with *lavash* or pitta bread.

3 lb (1½kg) chicken, oven ready
    with giblets removed
1 carrot, washed, peeled and thinly
    sliced
1 large onion, finely sliced
1 stalk celery, sliced into ½ inch
    (1cm) pieces

½ pint (300ml) yoghurt
2 eggs
1 teaspoon salt
½ teaspoon pepper
1 teaspoon ground fennel
1 teaspoon marjoram

**1** Wash the chicken, put in a large saucepan or casserole, cover with 2½ pints (1½l) water and bring to the boil. Remove the scum as it appears.

**2** Add the carrot, onion and celery, and simmer until the chicken is tender, about 2 hours.

**3** Remove the chicken from the stock, leave to cool; then remove the flesh and cut it into thin strips.

**4** Strain the stock, discard the vegetables and return the stock to the pan.

**5** Add the chicken.

**6** Whisk the yoghurt with the eggs in a bowl.

**7** Add a few tablespoons of the stock, salt, pepper and stir well.

**8** Add the yoghurt mixture to the pan and, stirring constantly, heat through but do not allow to boil.

**9** Serve hot, sprinkled with the fennel and marjoram.

## DUCK SOUP

This soup comes from Russia, where soured cream is traditionally used rather than yoghurt. I have found that yoghurt is just as good as, if not better than, soured cream. The redcurrant jelly and red wine give the soup a very attractive appearance.

*2 pints (1¼l) duck stock (chicken stock will do)*

*1 tablespoon redcurrant jelly*

*¼ pint (150ml) dry red wine*

*1 oz (25g) butter*

*2 shallots, chopped (spring onions, finely chopped, can be substituted)*

*1 teaspoon grated lemon rind*

*½ lb (250g) duck meat, cooked and finely chopped*

*½ teaspoon salt*

*½ teaspoon pepper*

*¼ pint (150ml) yoghurt*

*1 egg*

*1 teaspoon finely chopped lemon verbena (optional)*

**1** In a large saucepan first bring the stock to the boil.

**2** Stir in the redcurrant jelly and wine.

**3** Stir well and boil for 5 to 8 minutes.

**4** In another, smaller pan melt the butter, put in the shallots (or spring onions) and sauté for 2 minutes.

**5** Add the lemon rind and meat and cook for 5 more minutes.

6  Stir this mixture into the pan of stock, add the salt and pepper and stir thoroughly.

7  Put the yoghurt into a small bowl with the egg and beat thoroughly.

8  Add a tablespoon of the hot stock to the yoghurt and then add the mixture to the soup.

9  Stir constantly until the soup has thickened, but do not boil.

10  Before serving garnish with lemon verbena.

11  Serve immediately.

### SOUP-E-AROOSI
*Wedding soup*

This is a Turcoman dish, popular in Turkey and Iranian Azerbaijan. It is, as the name suggests, the soup of any village wedding. Simple and tasty.

| | |
|---|---|
| 2 oz (50g) butter | 2–3 teaspoons salt |
| 1 onion, thinly sliced | ½ teaspoon black pepper |
| 1 lb (½kg) lean lamb, cut into 1 in (3cm) pieces (beef can be substituted for the lamb) | 2 eggs |
| | 1 tablespoon lemon juice |
| | 2 tablespoons yoghurt |

1  In a large saucepan melt the butter and sauté the onion in the butter until golden brown.

2  Add the meat and sauté for 5 to 8 minutes or until nicely browned.

3  Add 3 pints (1¾l) water and simmer for ½ hour or until meat is tender, removing any scum which may appear on the surface.

4  Add the salt and pepper and mix well.

5  In a small bowl beat together the eggs, lemon juice and yoghurt.

6  Stir 3 tablespoons of the stock into the yoghurt mixture and then 3 more.

7  Pour the yoghurt mixture into the soup, taste and adjust seasoning if necessary.

8  Serve immediately.

## PUNJABI LENTIL SOUP

Lentils, turmeric and cumin powder give this soup a rich, earthy flavour. It is simple, nutritious and easy to make. Use red lentils for extra colour.

*6 oz (175g) whole lentils, cleaned and washed*
*2 tablespoons vegetable oil*
*1 onion, peeled and chopped*
*1–2 cloves garlic, finely chopped*
*1 teaspoon ground turmeric*

*½ teaspoon chilli powder*
*1 teaspoon salt*
*½ teaspoon black pepper*
*½ pint (300ml) yoghurt*
*cumin powder for garnish*

1  Soak the lentils for an hour in warm water.

2  In a saucepan heat the oil and sauté the onion and garlic until golden brown.

3  Drain the lentils and add the onion.

4  Add the turmeric, chilli powder, salt and pepper, and 2 pints (1¼l) water. Bring to the boil, lower the heat and simmer.

5  Cover the pan and cook for about an hour or until the lentils are cooked.

6  Gently stir in the yoghurt and leave long enough for the soup to heat through, but do not boil.

7  Serve immediately in soup bowls with a sprinkling of cumin.

## SPAS
### *Barley soup with dried yoghurt*

A classic of the Armenian cuisine. Traditionally prepared with *chortan* (p. 20). However, natural yoghurt will do just as well.

*3 oz (75g) pearl barley*
*¾ pint (450ml) plain yoghurt or 2 chortan balls*
*4 eggs*
*½ oz (15g) flour*
*1 small onion, finely chopped*
*1 oz (25g) butter*

*2 teaspoons salt*
*1 level teaspoon ground black pepper*
*2 teaspoons mint, finely chopped*
*2 teaspoons parsley or coriander leaves, finely chopped*

1  Soak barley in cold water overnight.
2  Drain barley and put in a large saucepan with about 2 pints (1¼l) water and cook for ½ hour or until tender.
3  Drain through a fine sieve.
4  Put yoghurt into a large bowl, add 2 pints (1¼l) water and mix until well blended. If you are using *chortan* balls, break them with a knife and mix with 3 pints (1¾l) water.
5  Break the eggs into a saucepan and whisk in the flour, a little at a time.
6  Stir in the yoghurt (or *chortan*) mixture and put over a moderate heat.
7  Whisk constantly in one direction to prevent curdling, bring almost to the boil and then lower the heat quickly.
8  Allow to simmer very gently for 2 to 3 minutes until the mixture thickens slightly.
9  Meanwhile melt the butter in a small pan and fry the onion until soft and just beginning to brown.
10  Stir the barley, cooked onion, salt and black pepper into the soup and simmer for another minute.
11  When ready to serve, sprinkle with the finely chopped fresh herbs.

### Printzov tanabour

*Rice yoghurt soup*

Follow the above recipe but use rice instead of barley. There is no need to soak the rice, simply wash it thoroughly and then cook and drain when tender. This soup has a reputation for being beneficial to the sick and those with stomach troubles.

### Chicken and barley soup with yoghurt

Follow the recipe for *spas* but use 3 pints (1¾l) chicken stock instead of water.

### ASH-E-JO
*Barley soup*

A thick wholesome soup of barley, vegetables and yoghurt from northern Iran, beloved by the Kurds and Turks of the region. Serve with bread.

| | |
|---|---|
| *2 oz (50g) red kidney beans* | *3 oz (75g) barley* |
| *2 oz (50g) chick peas* | *1 cup spinach, chopped* |
| *4 oz (100g) whole brown lentils* | *1 cup parsley, chopped* |
| *2 teaspoons salt* | *1 cup leeks, chopped* |
| *black pepper to taste* | *½ cup fresh dill or coriander leaves,* |
| *½ teaspoon turmeric* | *chopped* |
| *1 oz (25g) butter* | *½ pint (300ml) yoghurt* |
| *1 onion, finely chopped* | |

**1** Soak the kidney beans and chick peas in water overnight.

**2** In a large saucepan put the chick peas, kidney beans, lentils, 2 pints (1¼l) water, and the salt, pepper and turmeric.

**3** Meanwhile melt the butter in a small pan and sauté the onion until it is soft and brown.

**4** Add the onion and barley to the saucepan.

**5** Bring to the boil and allow to simmer for 45 minutes to 1 hour.

**6** Add the chopped vegetables and herbs, and continue simmering for another 30 minutes or until the beans, barley and chick peas are tender. Add a little more water if necessary.

**7** Remove the soup from the heat and slowly stir in the yoghurt.

**8** Serve immediately.

### ASH-E-MAST
*Iranian yoghurt soup*

This soup, like most Iranian dishes, is rich and elaborate – more like a stew. It is very filling and, as an added bonus, it uses inexpensive ingredients. It is particularly popular with the Azerbaijani Turks.

| | |
|---|---|
| *1 oz (25g) chick peas* | *2 oz (50g) whole brown lentils* |
| *1 oz (25g) haricot beans* | *1 onion, finely chopped* |

6 oz (175g) stewing lamb or lamb
  shank
½ teaspoon turmeric
1 oz (25g) butter

1 teaspoon salt
2 oz (50g) rice, washed
1 pint (½l) yoghurt

**1** Soak the chick peas, haricot beans and lentils in cold water overnight.

**2** Melt the butter and sauté the onion until it is soft and golden brown.

**3** Add the meat and cook for 5 to 10 minutes, stirring occasionally.

**4** Drain and rinse the chick peas, beans and lentils, and add to the saucepan, together with the turmeric, salt and rice, and 4 pints (2l) water.

**5** Cover and simmer for 1½ hours.

**6** If all the ingredients are cooked, remove the pan from the heat. If not, then continue cooking, adding more water if necessary.

**7** When cooked, remove the meat from the soup and reduce to a pulp either with a blender or a mortar and pestle.

**8** Return the meat pulp to the soup, stir and adjust seasoning if necessary.

**9** Beat the yoghurt in a small bowl and stir some of the soup into it.

**10** Slowly pour the yoghurt into the soup, heat through without boiling and serve immediately.

### HALIM BADEMJAN
#### Aubergine soup

This thick soup from Iran is really a meal in itself, ideal on a cold winter's night. You can substitute two chicken breasts for the lamb if you like.

1 large aubergine
3 oz (75g) butter
2 medium onions, very finely
  chopped
1 lb (½kg) lamb, cut into 1½–2 in
  (4–5cm) pieces
1 oz (25g) chick peas, soaked in cold
  water overnight

1½ oz (40g) whole brown lentils,
  washed
3 oz (75g) long grain rice, washed
1 teaspoon turmeric
2 teaspoons salt
¼ teaspoon black pepper
½ pint (300ml) yoghurt
¼ teaspoon cinnamon

1 Cut the end off the aubergine, peel the aubergine and slice thinly.

2 Arrange slices on a large plate, sprinkle with salt and leave for 30 minutes.

3 Rinse under cold water and pat dry with kitchen paper.

4 Meanwhile melt 1 oz (25g) butter in a large saucepan and cook the onions until golden brown.

5 Add the meat, chick peas, lentils, rice, 1 pint (600ml) water, turmeric, salt and pepper.

6 Bring to the boil, cover and simmer for about an hour.

7 Melt the remaining 2 oz (50g) butter in a frying pan and sauté the aubergine slices until they are brown on both sides. Add more butter if necessary.

8 Add the aubergines to the soup, cover and simmer for a further 30 to 40 minutes, until everything, especially the chick peas, is tender.

9 With a slotted spoon remove the meat and aubergine pieces and place in a liquidizer.

10 Blend with just sufficient stock to form a thick paste.

11 Return the paste to the soup and stir well.

12 Remove the soup from the heat.

13 Stir in the yoghurt, sprinkle with cinnamon and serve immediately.

## DOVGA
### *Yoghurt soup with meat-balls*

A popular soup in Azerbaijan, USSR and northern Iran. *Dovga* is rich in flavour and is served hot with *lavash*, pitta or *naan* bread.

½ lb (250g) minced meat (beef or lamb)
1 onion, finely chopped
salt and black pepper to taste
1½ pints (1l) yoghurt
1 tablespoon flour
2 pints (1¼l) stock or water
1 oz (25g) basmati rice, washed
1½ cups chopped spinach

2 oz (50g) chick peas, soaked overnight, cooked in water until just tender and drained; alternatively, use drained tinned chick peas
3 tablespoons finely chopped parsley
2 spring onions, finely chopped
3 tablespoons fresh dill, chopped (or 1 tablespoon dried dill weed)

1  In a large bowl mix the meat, onion, salt and pepper.
2  Knead until well blended and smooth.
3  Make small walnut-sized balls and put on one side.
4  Pour the yoghurt into a large saucepan and add the flour, mixed with a little stock or water. Add the rest of the stock or water and beat until well blended.
5  Season with a little salt and pepper.
6  Add the meat-balls and rice; simmer on a low heat for 12 to 15 minutes, stirring gently and very frequently.
7  Add the spinach and the cooked chick peas and simmer for a further 10 to 12 minutes until the rice is cooked and the meat is tender.
8  Add the parsley, onion and dill, and cook for a further 5 minutes.
9  Serve immediately.

## TUTMAJ
### *Noodle yoghurt soup*

Another classic Armenian yoghurt soup. Traditionally made with *chortan* (see p. 20). Natural yoghurt can be used instead. This version uses home-made noodles but any form of traditional small pasta is suitable. Small balls of minced meat can be added too, to give more substance to the dish, which, with bread, is often eaten as a main meal.

*1½ pints (1l) yoghurt*
*2 egg yolks*
*4–5 oz (125–150g) noodles*
*½ lb (250g) minced meat, seasoned and shaped into small marble-sized rissoles and fried (optional)*

*1 teaspoon salt*
*½ teaspoon pepper*
*1 onion, finely chopped*
*2 oz (50g) butter*
*2 tablespoons dried mint, crushed*

1  In a large pan bring the yoghurt and the egg yolks slowly to the boil, beating constantly.
2  Pour in ¾ pint (½l) water and add the noodles – also the fried meat-balls if you are including them.
3  Add the salt and pepper, bring to the boil, lower the heat and simmer for 8 to 10 minutes until the pasta is just cooked.
4  Meanwhile fry the onions in the butter.

5 Add the mint to the onions, stir, fry a little longer and then remove from the heat.

6 Pour the onion mixture into the soup. Stir well.

7 Serve immediately.

## MADZOONOV KUFTE
### *Wheat and meat-balls in yoghurt sauce*

A regional speciality from the city of Gazi-Antab in southern Turkey. Popular also with Syrians, who call it *Kibbeh-bi-laban*.

This is more than a soup, more of a meal when served with pickles and bread. Instead of the chicken you can use 3 lb (1½kg) lamb or beef cut into 2 in (5cm) cubes.

SERVES SIX TO EIGHT

*½ lb (250g) fresh lamb's suet from around the kidneys or ½ lb (250g) butter*

*3 lb (1½kg) chicken, cut into joints*

*4 oz (100g) chick peas, soaked overnight*

*3 teaspoons salt*

*2–2½ pints (1¼–1½l) yoghurt*

*2 eggs*

*2 oz (50g) butter*

*1 tablespoon dried mint*

KUFTE

*9 oz (275g) fine burghul (see p. 197)*

*12 oz (350g) lean lamb, minced twice*

*1 onion, finely chopped*

*2 teaspoons salt*

*1 teaspoon chilli powder*

1 Divide the fat into small pieces about the size of a pea, roll each one between the palms to form small balls and refrigerate.

2 Half fill a large saucepan with water, add the chicken joints, and chick peas and bring to the boil.

3 Remove any scum that gathers on the surface.

4 Cook until the meat and chick peas are tender, at least 1 hour. Season with the salt.

5 Meanwhile prepare the *kufte*. Wash the *burghul*, pour away excess water and spread the *burghul* on a baking sheet for about 10 minutes.

6 Add the minced meat, onion, salt, chilli powder and 2 tablespoons of cold water, and mix well.

7 Knead the mixture by placing both your hands on it and, taking hold of two handfuls, squeezing, pressing down and pushing it away from you. Repeat this several times.

8  Gather the mixture up into a ball in the middle of the baking sheet and knead again in the same way. Repeat several times.

9  Knead the mixture until it is well blended and smooth. It should take about 10 to 15 minutes. You will find it much easier if you sprinkle some water over it occasionally and keep your hands damp.

10  Break off small pieces of the *kufte* about the size of a walnut and roll between the palms to make balls.

11  Make a hole inside each with your forefinger. The simplest way to do this is to hold the ball of *kufte* in one hand, push the forefinger of the other hand inside the ball and press all around the wall, turning the ball while pressing.

12  Put a ball of suet into the hole.

13  Bring the edges of the opening together and seal.

14  Now roll the ball between your palms to give it a round shape and smooth outer surface.

15  Repeat this with all the *kufte*, occasionally dipping your hands into water to avoid them sticking.

16  When the suet is finished up simply make small marble-sized *kufte* balls without fillings.

17  Mix the yoghurt and eggs together in a small bowl.

18  Add a little of the hot chicken stock to the yoghurt and stir it in.

19  Add the yoghurt sauce to the large pan of stock, with the chicken and chick peas.

20  Simmer very gently.

21  In a small saucepan melt the butter, add the mint, stirring for 1 to 2 minutes and pour into the yoghurt soup.

22  Add the *kufte* balls to the soup and simmer, very gently, for 10 to 15 minutes until the *kufte* is cooked.

23  Serve hot, placing several *kufte* in each bowl with some of the chick peas and chicken and plenty of the liquid.

## MANTABOUR
### *Dumplings in a yoghurt soup*

This is a fascinating soup from Anatolia which, in fact, originated in China and Korea. *Manta* is a Chinese dumpling similar to ravioli, and was probably brought to the Middle East by the Mongolian tribes in their search for pastures.

SERVES SIX
DOUGH
*12 oz (350g) plain flour*
*1 egg*
*1 oz (25g) melted butter*
*½ teaspoon salt*

FILLING
*¾ lb (350g) minced lamb or beef*
*1 large onion, finely chopped*
*2 tablespoons finely chopped parsley*

*1 teaspoon salt*
*½ teaspoon black pepper*

SOUP
*3–4 pints (1¾–2¼l) stock*
*salt and pepper to taste*
*2 oz (50g) butter*
*1 large onion, finely chopped*
*1 tablespoon dried mint*
*1½ pints (1l) yoghurt*
*2 eggs*

1 Place the flour in a large mixing bowl and make a hollow in the middle.

2 Add the egg, butter, ⅓ pint (200ml) water and salt, and knead for 10 to 15 minutes until the dough is soft and elastic.

3 Shape the dough into a ball, cover with a tea-towel and leave to rest for 30 to 40 minutes.

4 Place all the ingredients for the filling in another bowl and knead well with damp hands.

5 For ease in handling divide the dough into two or three parts.

6 Flour a working top and roll out one part of the dough until paper thin.

7 Cut the pastry into 2 in (5cm) squares.

8 Repeat with the remaining dough.

9 Place a small ball of the meat mixture about the size of a cherry on a square.

10 Dip a finger in cold water and moisten the edges of the square.

11 Fold the pastry over to form a triangle and pinch the edges together to seal.

12 Keeping your fingers moist bring the two folded corners together and pinch firmly.

13 Repeat with the remaining squares of dough. If there is any meat mixture left over form into small balls and cook with the dumplings.

14 The alternative way of shaping the dumplings is to cut the pastry in 2 in (5cm) circles, place a little of the meat mixture in the centre and then bring the pastry up around the meat, collect the edges together and pinch to seal – thus forming small bags.

15 Bring the stock to the boil in a large saucepan and season with salt and pepper to taste.

16 Add the dumplings and simmer for 15 to 20 minutes until tender.

**17** In a small saucepan melt the butter and sauté the onion until golden brown.

**18** Stir in the mint and remove from the heat.

**19** Pour the yoghurt into a large bowl and beat in the eggs.

**20** Spoon about 1 pint (½l) of the boiling stock into the yoghurt and stir well.

**21** Slowly pour the yoghurt mixture into the large saucepan, stir and cook for 5 to 10 minutes, but do not let it boil.

**22** Add the onion mixture, cook for a further 2 to 3 minutes and then serve immediately.

# APPETIZERS

## APPLE AND CELERY CREAM

A simple and delightful hors d'oeuvre with celery giving it bite.

3 red eating apples
3 sticks of celery
1 tablespoon chopped chervil
1 teaspoon finely chopped parsley

1/4 pint (150ml) yoghurt
2 1/2 fl oz (75ml) double cream
1 teaspoon allspice for garnish

1 Core the apples.
2 Either mince the apples and celery in a mincer or chop very finely.
3 Place in a bowl and stir in the chervil and parsley.
4 Beat the yoghurt and cream together, pour over the salad and mix.
5 Serve the salad in individual dishes, sprinkled with a little allspice.


## ARTICHOKES WITH YOGHURT

Though normally a bland vegetable, with yoghurt and spices artichoke acquires a very good flavour.

juice of 1 lemon (retain the skin)
4 small artichokes
1/4 pint (150ml) olive oil
1 teaspoon coriander seeds

1 teaspoon marjoram
1 teaspoon basil
salt and pepper to taste
1/2 pint (300ml) yoghurt

1 Half fill a large saucepan with water, add 2 teaspoons lemon juice and bring to the boil. Leave simmering gently while you prepare the artichokes.
2 Cut the stalks from the artichokes and remove any coarse outer leaves.

3 Slice off the top third of each artichoke and discard.

4 Rub the inside of the lemon skin over the cut edges.

5 With kitchen scissors snip ¼ in (½cm) off the top of the remaining leaves and rub the cut edges again with the lemon skin.

6 Drop the artichokes into the simmering water and parboil for about 10 minutes.

7 Drain them, plunge into cold water and drain again.

8 Put 1 pint (600ml) water into a saucepan with the oil, lemon juice, coriander seeds, marjoram, basil and salt and pepper, and bring to the boil.

9 Add the artichokes and cook uncovered for a further 20 to 30 minutes. They are cooked when the bases can be pierced easily with a sharp knife.

10 Drain the artichokes but retain the juices and when cool enough to handle spread out the top leaves and pull out the prickly leaves surrounding the hairy choke.

11 With a teaspoon scrape out the choke and discard, then press the leaves back together again.

12 Place in the refrigerator to chill.

13 Before serving beat the yoghurt and stir in the reserved juices.

14 When ready to serve place the artichokes in small bowls and spoon the yoghurt sauce over the top of each.

## MADZNOV SUMPOOGI AGHTSAN
### *Aubergine purée with yoghurt*

A traditional Armenian recipe. It is ideal as an appetizer to be eaten with warm pitta or *lavash*. You can vary the number of chillies according to taste.

| | |
|---|---|
| *3 large aubergines* | *½ pint (300ml) yoghurt* |
| *2 fl oz (60ml) olive oil* | *6 green chillies* |
| *1 tablespoon lemon juice* | *3 cloves garlic* |
| *salt to taste* | *1 tablespoon finely chopped parsley* |

1 Pierce each aubergine a few times with a sharp knife.

2 Either place them on one of the shelves in the centre of a hot oven or place on skewers and grill over a charcoal fire.

3 Cook until they are soft when poked with a finger.

4 Allow to cool; cut off stems and peel off the skin.

5 Cut the flesh into pieces.

6 Heat the olive oil in a frying pan, add the aubergine flesh and fry for a few minutes.

7 Place the flesh in a large bowl, add the lemon juice, salt and yoghurt, and mash with a fork until smooth. Leave to cool.

8 Cook the green chillies under the grill, turning until cooked on all sides.

9 Cut the stalk ends off and remove the skins from three, setting the other three aside.

10 In a mortar crush the chillies and garlic with ½ teaspoon of salt until smooth.

11 Stir into the aubergine mixture.

12 Spread the purée over a large plate.

13 Remove the skin from the remaining chillies, chop coarsely and use to garnish the salad, together with the chopped parsley.

### DABGEVADZ SUMPOOG
*Fried aubergine with yoghurt*

A traditional recipe from Cilician Armenia, this is popular throughout Turkey and Syria as well. Apart from being a tasty appetizer it also makes a good side dish for lamb kebab.

> *2 large aubergines*
> *salt*
> *olive or vegetable oil*
> *½ pint (300ml) garlic yoghurt sauce (see p. 167)*
> *1 teaspoon dried mint*

1 Slice the heads and tails from the aubergines.

2 Cut the aubergines crosswise into ½ in (1cm) slices.

3 Arrange slices on a large plate, sprinkle with salt and leave for ½ hour.

4 Rinse under cold water and dry on kitchen paper.

5 Pour some oil into a large saucepan or frying pan and heat.

6 Fry some of the aubergine slices on both sides until a light golden brown. Remove to absorbant kitchen paper.

7 Repeat with the remaining slices.

**8** Arrange half the slices over a large plate.

**9** Pour some of the yoghurt sauce over them and arrange the remaining slices on top.

**10** Pour the rest of the yoghurt over the top and sprinkle with the mint.

### Kabak tavasi
*Fried courgettes*

A Turkish-Armenian variation.

| | |
|---|---|
| *4 courgettes, topped, tailed and sliced crosswise into ½ in (1cm) pieces* | *oil* |
| | *½ pint (300ml) garlic yoghurt sauce* |
| | *mint* |

Prepare in the same way as the above.

## AVOCADO SALAD

A refreshing and attractive appetizer. You could also add pieces of *feta* cheese.

| | |
|---|---|
| *2 ripe avocados* | *1 slice melon, cut into cubes* |
| *salt* | *8 stuffed olives* |
| *½ grapefruit, separated into segments* | *¼ pint (150ml) Orga's yoghurt dressing (see p. 166)* |
| *1 tangerine, separated into segments* | |

**1** Cut the avocados in half lengthwise and remove the stones.

**2** Scoop out the flesh, cut into cubes and place in a large bowl. Reserve the shells.

**3** Sprinkle the avocado flesh with a little salt.

**4** Remove the skin from the grapefruit and tangerine segments and cut the flesh into pieces.

**5** Add to the bowl, together with the pieces of melon and the stuffed olives.

**6** Toss all the fruits together and refrigerate for a few hours.

**7** Prepare the yoghurt dressing.

**8** When ready to serve spoon the fruits into the avocado shells and pour a little of the dressing over each.

## BAKLA
### *Broad beans in yoghurt*

This is an adaptation of a Turkish–Kurdish dish. You can omit the spring onions and substitute finely sliced Spanish onions. Try garnishing it with sliced tomatoes and cucumber. Serve with pitta bread. It is a good accompaniment to all roast and cooked meat and fowl dishes.

*1 lb (½kg) broad beans (If you have young beans then do not shell them but use them as they are. Otherwise use 1 lb (½kg) shelled beans.)*
*2 teaspoons salt*
*1 tablespoon lemon juice*
*2 teaspoons chopped dill or 1 teaspoon dried dillweed*

*1 teaspoon chopped mint*
*1 teaspoon oregano*
*½ teaspoon black pepper*
*¼ pint (150ml) olive oil*
*4 spring onions or 1 Spanish onion*
*½ pint (300ml) garlic yoghurt sauce (see p. 167)*
*1 teaspoon cumin powder*
*½ teaspoon cayenne pepper*

**1** If using young beans and pods then cut off the tops and string the sides of the pods. Wash thoroughly and cut into 1 in (3cm) lengths. Otherwise simply wash the beans.

**2** Into a large saucepan put the beans, salt, lemon juice, dill, mint, oregano and black pepper.

**3** Meanwhile heat the oil in a small pan and fry the onions until soft.

**4** Add the onions and the oil to the large saucepan together with ½ pint (300ml) water.

**5** Cook for about an hour or until the beans are tender and the water has reduced substantially.

**6** Chill in the refrigerator for a few hours.

**7** Whisk the garlic yoghurt sauce and pour over the beans.

**8** Sprinkle with cumin powder and cayenne pepper.

**9** Serve cold as an appetizer.

## KASHK-E KADOO
### *Courgettes with yoghurt*

This Iranian appetizer is traditionally made with liquid whey, but I find that it works better with yoghurt. As well as being an

appetizer this makes a tasty vegetable dish to serve with lamb
or poultry.

*3 medium-to-large courgettes*
*1½ oz (40g) butter*
*1 onion, finely chopped*
*1 clove garlic, crushed*
*½ teaspoon turmeric*

*1 teaspoon salt*
*¾ pint (450ml) yoghurt, stabilized*
  *with 1 tablespoon flour*
*1 teaspoon dried mint*

**1** Remove heads and tails from the courgettes then cut each courgette into four lengthwise.

**2** Cut each quarter into ¼ in (½cm) pieces.

**3** Melt 1 oz (25g) butter in a saucepan, add the onion and garlic and sauté until the onion is golden brown.

**4** Add the courgettes and sauté, stirring occasionally for a few minutes.

**5** Stir in the turmeric, salt and 2½ fl oz (75ml) water and simmer, stirring occasionally, until the liquid has been absorbed and the courgettes are just tender.

**6** Very slowly stir in the yoghurt and heat through, but do not boil.

**7** Melt the remaining ½ oz (15g) butter in a small pan, add the mint and cook for 2 to 3 minutes.

**8** Spoon the courgettes and yoghurt into a serving dish and then pour the butter and mint mixture over the top.

**9** Serve immediately.

## TZAJIKI
### Cucumber and yoghurt dip

This Greek dip is similar to the Armenian *jajig* (see p. 65), with a few additional ingredients. Spread it over bread or biscuit, or serve it with hot pitta bread.

*½ cucumber, peeled*
*⅓ pint (200ml) yoghurt*
*1 clove garlic, finely chopped*
*2 tablespoons olive oil*
*1 teaspoon vinegar*

*1 tablespoon double cream*
*½ teaspoon icing sugar*
*salt and pepper to taste*
*1 tablespoon finely chopped mint or*
  *1 teaspoon dried mint*

1 Chop the cucumber very finely.
2 Place in a sieve and leave for ½ hour to drain.
3 In a bowl mix all the other ingredients, except the mint.
4 Dry the cucumber in a kitchen towel, then add to the yoghurt mixture and mix thoroughly.
5 Transfer to a salad bowl and sprinkle with mint.
6 Chill in the refrigerator for ½ to 1 hour.
7 Serve as a dip.

## KALEH JOOSH
### *Dates and walnuts with yoghurt*

This is an Iranian dish, also popular in Iraq. It is traditionally made with liquid whey (*kashk*) but yoghurt is an excellent substitute.

*1½ oz (40g) butter*
*1 onion, finely chopped*
*1 teaspoon dried mint*
*1 clove garlic, crushed*
*1 pint (600ml) yoghurt, stabilized*
*with 1 egg (see p. 17)*

*½ teaspoon saffron dissolved in 1*
*tablespoon boiling water*
*½ lb (250g) stoned dates, thinly*
*sliced lengthwise*
*2 oz (50g) walnuts, roughly chopped*

1 Melt the butter in a saucepan and sauté the onion, mint and garlic until the onion is soft.
2 Stir in the stabilized yoghurt, bring just to the boil and remove immediately from the heat.
3 Stir in the saffron, dates and walnuts.
4 Spoon into a serving dish.
5 Serve warm, with bread.

## FRUIT CUP

A tangy appetizer that makes an excellent use of fruits and yoghurt.

1 large grapefruit
2 oranges
1 tin pineapple chunks or 1 small
  fresh pineapple, peeled and cut
  into small cubes

½ pint (300ml) yoghurt
2 tablespoons sugar or 2 tablespoons
  honey
fresh mint leaves for garnish

1 Peel the grapefruit and oranges and divide the fruit into segments.

2 Remove the skin from the segments and then cut the fruit into small pieces.

3 Mix all the fruit in a large bowl and chill in the refrigerator for a few hours.

4 At the same time mix the yoghurt and sugar or honey together, and chill.

5 Spoon the fruit into a large glass bowl or into individual glasses and spoon the yoghurt over the fruit.

6 Garnish with fresh mint leaves and serve chilled.


## ZAKUSKA
### Mushrooms on toast

This popular and traditional Russian dish is normally served with soured cream, but yoghurt is an excellent substitute. As well as being a tasty appetizer, this makes a quickly prepared snack meal.

2 oz (50g) butter
4 spring onions, chopped
2 teaspoons paprika
1 lb (½kg) mushrooms, wiped clean
  and sliced thickly
1 tablespoon lemon juice
2 tablespoons flour

¾ pint (450ml) yoghurt
1 teaspoon salt
½ teaspoon black pepper
4 large slices wholewheat or rye
  bread
a little chopped fresh dill or parsley

1 Melt the butter in a saucepan and sauté the onions until soft.

2 Stir in the paprika and cook for 1 minute.

3 Add the mushrooms and lemon juice to the pan and sauté for about 5 minutes, stirring occasionally.

4 Add the flour and stir in well.

5 Add the yoghurt slowly, stirring constantly until the mixture thickens.

6 Season with the salt and pepper.

7 Meanwhile remove the crusts and then toast the slices of bread.

8 Cut each slice into four triangles and either arrange over a large serving plate or on individual plates.

9 Spoon the mushroom mixture over the toast and garnish with the fresh dill or parsley.

## SALAD E NOKHOD BA MAST
### Yoghurt and green pea salad

A delightful appetizer from Iran, where it is an integral part of any self-respecting buffet table. Scoop it up with bread or lettuce leaves.

1 lb (½kg) potatoes, preferably new

4 oz (125g) green peas, fresh or frozen

4 oz (125g) labna made from 1 pint (600ml) yoghurt (see p. 18)

3 tablespoons chopped fresh dill or 2 tablespoons dried dillweed

2 fl oz (60ml) olive oil

2 tablespoons lemon juice

2 dill pickles, thinly sliced

salt and pepper to taste

lettuce leaves

a few washed radishes for garnish

1 Boil the potatoes until tender, cool slightly, peel and cut into ½ in (1cm) cubes.

2 Cook the peas until tender.

3 Put the potatoes into a large salad bowl with the peas.

4 Mix in the labna, dill, olive oil, lemon juice, dill pickles, salt and pepper to taste.

5 Leave in the refrigerator to chill for a few hours.

6 Serve on lettuce leaves, garnished with a few radishes.

## PEAR COCKTAIL

An attractive starter or a cocktail dish which should go down well at parties.

2 large ripe pears
¼ pint (150ml) yoghurt
¼ teaspoon salt
a pinch of black pepper
a few drops Worcestershire sauce

2 tablespoons grated cheese (e.g.
   Cheddar, feta, Edam)
2 tablespoons chopped mixed nuts
a little paprika

1  Peel, halve and core the pears.
2  In a small bowl mix together the yoghurt, salt, pepper, Worcestershire sauce, cheese and nuts.
3  Spoon this mixture into the cavity of each pear half.
4  Chill and serve sprinkled with a little paprika.

## MADZNOV DAKDEGH
### Green peppers with yoghurt

Another Armenian appetizer; it is usually served cold spread on pitta or any other bread.

4 large green peppers
½ pint (300ml) garlic yoghurt sauce
   (see p. 167)

½ teaspoon cumin
½ teaspoon black pepper
3 tomatoes, quartered (optional)

1  Wash the green peppers and cut out the stems and seeds.
2  Cook under the grill (or over a charcoal fire if you have one going), turning occasionally until they are well cooked all over.
3  Remove from the heat and leave to cool.
4  Peel off the outer skins.
5  Quarter each pepper and then cut into very thin slices.
6  Arrange the slices in a serving dish and stir in the yoghurt sauce.
7  Sprinkle with the cumin and black pepper and decorate with the tomatoes if you wish.

## ZNONIT BESHAMENET
### Radishes with yoghurt

This Israeli salad is normally made with soured cream – it has East European origins. I have substituted natural yoghurt and have found that it is a great improvement.

3 teaspoons wine vinegar
1 teaspoon white sugar
1 teaspoon salt
½ teaspoon black pepper

½ pint (300ml) yoghurt
20 or so radishes
1 small onion

**1** Mix the vinegar, sugar, salt, pepper and yoghurt in a small bowl and leave in the refrigerator to chill.
**2** Trim and wash the radishes.
**3** Cut the radishes crosswise into thin slices.
**4** Peel the onion and cut crosswise into thin slices.
**5** Push the onion slices out into rings.
**6** Put the radishes and onion into a large salad bowl.
**7** Pour the dressing over the top and mix well.
**8** Refrigerate for an hour or so and serve well chilled.

## GARDOFILOV AGHTSAN
### *Potato and yoghurt appetizer*

A recipe from the Caucasus, popular with Armenians and Georgians. The dish is traditionally made with soured cream, but I have adapted it for yoghurt. It makes a fine appetizer or side salad.

1½ lb (¾kg) evenly sized potatoes
½ cucumber peeled and thinly sliced
2 shallots, finely chopped, or 2
   spring onions, finely sliced

T teaspoon salt
½ teaspoon black pepper
¼ pint (150ml) yoghurt
2 tablespoons finely chopped parsley

**1** Wash the potatoes and cook in boiling water.
**2** When tender drain, cool and peel.
**3** Cut the potatoes into ½ in (1cm) pieces and place in a large salad bowl.
**4** Add the cucumber slices and chopped onion.
**5** Gently stir in the salt, pepper and yoghurt and leave in the refrigerator for an hour.
**6** Serve sprinkled with the chopped parsley.

## SHOMIN
### *Spinach and yoghurt salad*

This is a classic of the Armenian cuisine. It is superb to look at with its dazzling combination of colours, and what is more it is simple to make. Serve it as an appetizer or as an accompaniment to roast and grilled meats.

*1 lb (½kg) fresh or frozen leaf*
  *spinach*
*2 oz (50g) butter*
*1 small onion, finely chopped*
*salt and black pepper to taste*

*½ pint (300ml) yoghurt*
*2 cloves garlic, crushed*
*paprika*
*2 tablespoons finely chopped toasted*
  *walnuts (optional)*

 1 Strip the leaves from the stalks of the fresh spinach and wash very thoroughly to remove all the grit and sand. (Thaw out frozen spinach.)

 2 Half fill a large pan with water, bring to the boil and add the spinach.

 3 Simmer for about 10 minutes or until the spinach is just cooked.

 4 Strain into a colander and leave until cool enough to handle.

 5 Using your hands, squeeze out as much of the water as possible.

 6 Chop the spinach.

 7 Melt the butter in a large frying pan and fry the onion until it is soft and just beginning to brown.

 8 Add the chopped spinach and fry for a further 5 minutes.

 9 Season to taste with the salt and black pepper.

10 Keep on a low heat while you mix the yoghurt and crushed garlic together in a small bowl.

11 Divide the spinach into four portions and arrange each on a small plate in a circular shape.

12 Spoon some of the yoghurt into the centre of each circle and then sprinkle the yoghurt with just a little paprika.

13 If you like, sprinkle a few chopped walnuts over the top.

## BORANI-YE-ESFENAG
### *Iranian spinach and yoghurt salad*

A simple, cheap and appetizing salad. It is related to the Armenian *shomin*, but here the yoghurt is tossed into the salad proper and it is served chilled. It is also an excellent accompaniment to meat dishes.

*½ lb (250g) spinach*
*2 tablespoons lemon juice*
*1 tablespoon finely chopped onion*
*½ teaspoon salt*

*a pinch of black pepper*
*½ pint (300ml) yoghurt*
*1 tablespoon finely chopped fresh*
  *mint or 1 teaspoon dried mint*

**1** Wash the spinach several times in cold water until all the sand and grit has been removed.

**2** Strip the leaves from the stalks and discard the stalks.

**3** Bring 1 pint (½l) water to the boil in a large saucepan.

**4** Add the spinach, lower the heat and simmer for about 10 minutes.

**5** Drain the spinach in a colander, allow to cool a little and then squeeze out between your palms.

**6** Chop the spinach finely and put it into a large salad bowl.

**7** Add the lemon juice, onion, salt and pepper.

**8** Toss with a wooden spoon.

**9** Add the yoghurt and mix thoroughly.

**10** Refrigerate for at least an hour.

**11** Serve with a garnish of mint.

### LABAN-BI-TAHINA

A popular Arab appetizer made of sesame seed paste and yoghurt; it is eaten throughout the Middle East and is traditionally served as an appetizer with thin bread or as an accompaniment to grilled fish or meat.

*½ pint (300ml) tahina (available*
  *from many healthfood shops)*
*2 cloves garlic, crushed*
*½ teaspoon salt*
*½ pint (300ml) yoghurt*

*juice of 2 lemons*
*pinch of ground cumin*
*pinch of paprika*
*1 tablespoon finely chopped parsley*

**1** Pour the *tahina* into a bowl, add the garlic and salt and mix well.

**2** Add the yoghurt and lemon juice and then beat vigorously for several minutes until you have a thick, smooth cream.

**3** Pour into a shallow bowl and sprinkle decoratively with the golden cumin and red paprika.

4 Garnish with the parsley, either scattered all over the surface or bunched together in the centre.

## TZOO-YEV-MADZOON

From Caucasian Armenia. This is a decorative dish of hard-boiled eggs on a bed of lettuce leaves with chopped vegetables and a delicious fresh-tasting dressing. It can be served either as an hors d'oeuvre or as the main dish for a summer lunch.

*1 round lettuce, coarse outer leaves*
*discarded, separated into leaves*
*and washed*
*8 hard-boiled eggs, shelled*
*8 black olives, halved and stoned*
*2 bunches watercress, washed and*
*shaken dry*
*10 large radishes, thinly sliced*
*1 large green pepper, seeded and*
*thinly sliced*
*3 medium carrots, scraped and*
*grated*

DRESSING
*½ pint (300ml) yoghurt*
*2 teaspoons lemon juice*
*1 teaspoon tarragon vinegar*
*2 tablespoons chopped fresh chives*
*1 teaspoon dried dillweed*
*1 tablespoon chopped parsley*
*1 teaspoon paprika*
*½ teaspoon salt*
*¼ teaspoon black pepper*

1 Arrange the lettuce leaves on a large serving platter.

2 Slice the eggs in half lengthways and then place them around the edge of the platter, cut side downwards.

3 Top each half egg with half an olive.

4 Divide the watercress into sixteen equal portions and arrange them in the spaces between the eggs, with the stems pointing inwards.

5 Mix the radishes, green pepper and carrots together in a bowl.

6 Pile the mixture into the middle of the ring made by the eggs.

7 Combine all the ingredients for the sauce together in a small bowl and beat thoroughly.

8 Pour into a sauce-boat and serve with the salad.

## BULZ GĂTIŢI CU OUĂ
### *Fried dumplings filled with butter and cheese*

This is a classic Romanian dish made with polenta (maize flour), which is also popular in Italian cuisine. Although usually served with soured cream, try topping them with yoghurt instead. They are a little difficult to make, but you will find that they will be worth the effort.

They can be served as a starter or as a light main course.

*6 oz (175g) polenta*
*1½ teaspoons salt*
*6½-in (1cm) cubes hard butter*
*6½-in (1cm) cubes strong, hard*

*cheese, e.g.* haloumi, *Cheddar or*
*Parmesan*
*2 oz (50g) butter*
*½ pint (300ml) yoghurt*

**1** Put the polenta and salt into a large saucepan with 1 pint (600ml) water.

**2** Bring to the boil, stirring continuously, and cook for a further 5 to 8 minutes, still stirring, until the mixture is very thick.

**3** Pour the mixture on to a plate and leave until it is completely cold.

**4** Divide the mixture into six and flatten with your hands into cakes roughly round in shape.

**5** Put a cube of butter and cheese into the centre of each.

**6** Wet your hands and then shape each cake into a round dumpling, making sure that the filling is completely enclosed.

**7** Heat the grill to red hot and then melt 2 oz (50g) butter in the grill pan.

**8** Place the dumplings in the pan and roll them in the butter until completely coated.

**9** Grill for about 10 minutes, turning once.

**10** Serve immediately with any remaining butter in the grill pan poured over the dumplings; top with the yoghurt.

## PRAWN COCKTAIL WITH YOGHURT

The ever-popular prawn cocktail with a difference. The flavour of yoghurt gives it a new dimension.

*½ pint (300ml) yoghurt*
*2–3 tablespoons mayonnaise*

*1 tablespoon tomato purée*
*a few drops tabasco*

½ teaspoon salt
¼ teaspoon black pepper
lettuce leaves, washed, shaken and
  finely shredded

1 lb (½kg) prawns – if frozen thaw
  them out
lemon wedges

1 In a bowl mix the yoghurt, mayonnaise, tomato purée, tabasco, salt and pepper, and chill in the refrigerator.

2 When ready to serve arrange shredded lettuce in individual bowls or plates and place the prawns on top.

3 Spoon the yoghurt sauce over the prawns.

4 Serve a large lemon wedge with each portion.


## SALTED HERRINGS WITH YOGHURT

This is a recipe from Irfan Orga's book *Cooking with Yogurt*. It makes a marvellous hors d'oeuvre.

4 fillets of salted herring
6 soft herring roes
1 tablespoon tarragon vinegar
6 tablespoons yoghurt

½ teaspoon finely chopped onion
½ teaspoon chervil
½ teaspoon chives
½ teaspoon tarragon

1 Soak the herring fillets in cold water for an hour and then drain.

2 Arrange them on a large serving dish.

3 In a small bowl mash the roes with the vinegar and yoghurt.

4 Stir in the onion and herbs.

5 Pour this mixture over the herrings and chill until ready to serve. It is best served very cold.

# SALADS

### ASBOURAG AGHTSAN
*Asparagus and yoghurt salad*

This is an old recipe dating from the tenth century. It is a highly sophisticated combination of asparagus and yoghurt with the added flavour of garlic.

*1 lb (½kg) fresh asparagus*
*1½ teaspoons salt*
*1 pint (600ml) yoghurt*
*1 teaspoon dried mint*

*1–2 cloves garlic (depending on taste), crushed*
*1 spring onion, finely sliced*
*1 hard-boiled egg, chopped*

1 Remove the tough white part at the bottom of each asparagus stalk. You will achieve a more even effect if you cut them rather than snap them off.

2 Cut stalks into 1 in (3cm) pieces.

3 Put into a large saucepan, just cover with water, add 1 teaspoon of salt and bring to the boil.

4 Simmer for about 10 minutes or until just tender. Do not overcook.

5 Drain the asparagus and leave to cool.

6 Pour the yoghurt into a small bowl and stir in the garlic, ½ teaspoon salt, mint and onion until well blended.

7 Gently stir the chopped egg through the sauce.

8 Place the asparagus in a serving bowl and spoon the sauce over the top.

9 Serve cold, with roast meat or poultry or cold meat cuts.

## BAIGAN PACHCHADI
### *Spiced aubergines with yoghurt*

This comes from North India, where there are several such vegetable dishes cooked with mustard seeds, chillies and yoghurt. Courgettes, okra, spinach, turnips, etc. can be substituted for the aubergine. Serve with meat and poultry dishes as well as with dry curry dishes.

3 tablespoons oil
1 teaspoon black mustard seeds
1 onion, finely chopped
2 fresh green chillies, seeded and
  sliced
1 medium aubergine, peeled and
  diced
1 tomato, chopped

1 teaspoon salt
1 teaspoon garam masala
  (see p. 197)
½ teaspoon chilli powder (optional)
½ pint (300ml) yoghurt
2 tablespoons chopped fresh
  coriander leaves

1 Heat the oil in a saucepan and fry the mustard seeds until they pop.

2 Add the onions and chillies, and fry until the onion is soft.

3 Add the aubergine and fry for a few minutes, stirring frequently.

4 Stir in the tomato, salt, *garam masala* and chilli powder.

5 Add 2 fl oz (60ml) water, stir well, cover and cook until the aubergine and tomato can be mashed to a purée.

6 Cool, stir in the yoghurt and half of the chopped coriander leaves.

7 Serve garnished with the remaining leaves.

## AVOCADO IM EGOZIM
### *Avocado and walnut salad*

This Israeli salad uses avocado, walnuts and yoghurt, which, strange as it may seem, go very well together. It is an ideal accompaniment to all kinds of roast or grilled meats.

2 ripe avocados
juice of 1 lime (or lemon)
4 spring onions, finely sliced,
  including heads
2 dill pickles, thinly sliced

1 stick celery, finely chopped
2 oz (50g) walnuts, chopped
1 teaspoon salt
¼ teaspoon black pepper
2 tablespoons chopped parsley

¼ *pint (150ml) yoghurt – or more*    ½ *teaspoon dillweed*
  *depending on taste*                *24 black olives*

**1** Cut the avocados in half, lengthwise, remove the stones and carefully scoop out the flesh.

**2** Cube the flesh and place in a large salad bowl.

**3** Sprinkle with the lime or lemon juice and add the spring onions, dill pickles, celery and walnuts.

**4** Season with the salt, pepper and parsley, and toss.

**5** Stir in the yoghurt and then refrigerate for at least 1 hour.

**6** Before serving sprinkle with the dill and garnish with the black olives.

## MADZOUNOV SHAGHGAM
### *Beetroot and yoghurt salad*

This Armenian salad is popular throughout the Caucasus and northern Iran. It makes a good accompaniment to roast meats and chicken.

*1 lb (½kg) beetroot, washed; remove*    *1 onion, finely chopped*
  *the tops but do not cut the skin* (or   ½ *pint (300ml) garlic yoghurt sauce*
  *use tinned beetroot)*                 *(see p. 167)*
*1 oz (25g) butter*

**1** Cook the beetroot in lightly salted boiling water for about 1 hour or until tender.

**2** Drain, dip in cold water and rub off the skins.

**3** Melt the butter in a small saucepan and sauté the onion until golden brown.

**4** Dice the beetroot and add to the saucepan.

**5** Keep warm until ready to serve.

**6** Arrange in a dish and pour the yoghurt sauce over the top.

### A Greek variation

**1** Follow the above recipe up to the end of step 4.

**2** Stir in the garlic yoghurt sauce, 3 tablespoons white wine and 1 teaspoon sugar.

3  Heat through but do not boil.

4  Spoon into a serving dish and sprinkle with a little chopped parsley.


### An Arabic variation

Here the butter and onion are omitted and the diced beetroot is tossed in lemon juice and olive oil and then garnished with a little chopped parsley.


## MADZNA-GAGHAMP
### *Cabbage and olive salad with yoghurt*

This is my adaptation of an Armenian salad. The white cabbage is traditionally pickled in a marinade for several days until it turns red. You may use red cabbage but it will lack the sharp, biting flavour of marinated cabbage.

¾ lb (350g) cabbage, preferably pickled (see below)

1 onion, finely chopped

2 apples, peeled, cored and cut into small cubes

a small bunch of grapes, separated and washed

20 black olives, stoned and halved

2 tablespoons walnuts, coarsely chopped

1 teaspoon salt

½ pint (300ml) yoghurt

1 teaspoon oregano

fresh tarragon leaves or watercress as a garnish

1  Chop the cabbage leaves coarsely.

2  Place the cabbage in a large bowl together with the onion, apples, grapes, olives, walnuts and salt.

3  Toss the salad lightly and chill for at least 1 hour.

4  To serve the salad arrange it in a pyramid shape on a flat plate.

5  Whisk the yoghurt until it is frothy.

6  Pour the yoghurt over the salad.

7  Sprinkle the oregano over the top and garnish with the tarragon or watercress leaves.

## Pickled cabbage

If you would like to pickle cabbage in the Armenian way then try this simple method.

1 Put the cabbage into a large saucepan or casserole and cover with cold water.

2 Bring to the boil and simmer for about 45 minutes or until tender.

3 Drain and chop the leaves coarsely.

4 Put the cabbage in a large bowl, preferably glass or earthenware, and add:

*2 lb (1kg) beetroot, peeled and cubed*
*a few sprigs parsley*
*1 bunch green celery leaves*
*1 pint (600ml) wine vinegar*

*2 teaspoons paprika*
*sufficient water to cover by 2–3 ins*
   *(5–8cm)*

5 Place a plate with a weight on it over the cabbage to keep it under the marinade. If the weight is metal it should be wrapped in foil.

6 Leave to pickle for 1 week.

7 By the end of the week the cabbage will have turned deep red and have a piquant flavour.

## GAROSI AGHTSAN
### *Celery and walnuts with sweet yoghurt*

This Caucasian salad is a good accompaniment to pork or poultry roasts and kebabs. If you cannot find quinces use eating apples instead.

*3 sticks celery*
*2 quinces or 3 eating apples*
*½ pint (300ml) yoghurt*
*2 tablespoons liquid honey*

*2 tablespoons chopped walnuts*
*a few drops lemon juice*
*1 tablespoon chopped parsley*

1 Wash the celery thoroughly and cut into ¼ in (½cm) pieces.

2 Peel and core the quinces or apples and chop them into ½ in (1cm) cubes.

3 Pour the yoghurt into a bowl and whisk until frothy, add the honey and continue whisking.

4 Sprinkle the walnuts into the yoghurt.

**5** Arrange the celery and quinces in a serving bowl and pour the yoghurt sauce over them.

**6** Sprinkle with lemon juice and chopped parsley and serve.


### Variation

Grated carrot with eating apples and yoghurt and honey dressing also makes a tasty salad. Use the same quantities and method.


### JAJIG
*Cucumber and yoghurt salad with garlic and salt*

*Çaçuk* in Turkey, *tzajiki* in Greece and the Balkans, *mast-khiar* in Iran, *khira raita* in India, *khiar-bi-laban* in Arab lands and *jajig* in Armenia, this simple salad is perhaps the best known yoghurt-based salad of all. Simple and versatile, it can be served with any dish. If you add 1 pint (½l) water to it, you get a cool, refreshing soup.

*1 pint (½l) yoghurt*
*½ teaspoon salt*
*1 clove garlic, crushed*
*1 cucumber, peeled and diced*

*1 tablespoon finely chopped fresh*
*mint or 1 teaspoon dried mint*
*a pinch of chilli powder as a*
*garnish.*

**1** Place the yoghurt in a mixing bowl.

**2** Stir in the salt, garlic, cucumber and mint and mix well.

**3** Place in the refrigerator to chill until ready to serve.

**4** Pour into individual side dishes and sprinkle with the chilli powder.


### Biberli çaçuk
*Yoghurt and pepper salad*

A regional speciality from Marisa, Turkey. The quantities are as for *jajig*, but substitute 3 tablespoons finely chopped parsley for the mint and omit the chilli powder.

1  Grill 6 small green hot peppers, turning twice. Allow to cool, peel off the skin and remove the seeds.

2  Cut the peppers into small pieces about ¼ in (½cm) square.

3  Place the yoghurt in a mixing bowl.

4  Stir in salt, garlic, chopped peppers, 3 tablespoons finely chopped parsley and 1 clove garlic thinly sliced. Mix well.

5  Serve in individual side dishes with 1 teaspoon of olive oil on top.

## VELLARIKAI PACHCHADI
### *Indian cucumber and yoghurt salad*

This may be served as an accompaniment to any curry. If fresh coconut is not available use desiccated coconut soaked in half the yoghurt for 30 minutes and then blend in as directed.
A rather hot salad – be warned!

| | |
|---|---|
| 1 cucumber, peeled and finely chopped | ¾ pint (450ml) yoghurt |
| | 1 teaspoon salt |
| ½ fresh coconut or 1 oz (25g) desiccated coconut | 2 teaspoons vegetable oil |
| | 1 teaspoon mustard seeds |
| 2 green chillies, seeded | |

1  Place the chopped cucumber in a colander and set aside to drain for 1 hour.

2  With a sharp knife pare off the thin brown skin of the coconut and cut the flesh into pieces.

3  Put the coconut pieces and chillies into a blender.

4  Add 2–3 tablespoons of water and blend until a smooth purée is formed.

5  Add more water if necessary.

6  Scrape the purée into a medium-sized serving bowl.

7  Beat in the yoghurt, cucumber and salt.

8  In a small frying pan heat the oil and fry the mustard seeds until they pop.

9  Stir the mustard seeds and the oil into the yoghurt mixture.

10  Cover the bowl and chill until ready to serve.

## MANGO RAETA
### *Mangoes in yoghurt*

From northern India, this salad can be served with curries, roasts and grilled meats. *Raeta* means 'vegetable with curd' and virtually any vegetables can be prepared in this way. The more popular ones are banana, cucumber, onion and potato, aubergine and mango – the recipe for which is given below.

*1 pint (½l) yoghurt*
*2 ripe, fresh mangoes, peeled, stoned and diced (If fresh mangoes are not available canned ones can be used.)*
*½ teaspoon salt*

*1 tablespoon ghee (see p. 197) or clarified butter*
*1 tablespoon mustard seeds*
*1 green chilli, finely chopped*
*2 teaspoons finely chopped coriander leaves or parsley*

1 In a mixing bowl beat the yoghurt until smooth.
2 Add the mangoes and salt, stir and set aside.
3 In a small pan melt the ghee and when it is hot add the mustard seeds and fry until the seeds begin to pop.
4 Add the chilli and fry, stirring constantly, for 10 seconds.
5 Tip the contents of the pan into the yoghurt mixture and stir well.
6 Cover the mixture and chill.
7 Before serving sprinkle with the coriander leaves.

### Kela raeta
#### *Banana in yoghurt*

Very good with meat and chicken curries.

*1 pint (½l) yoghurt*
*3 bananas, thinly sliced*
*½ teaspoon salt*

*1 green chilli, finely chopped*
*2 teaspoons finely chopped coriander leaves or parsley*

1 Beat the yoghurt with salt, until smooth.
2 Add the bananas and chilli.
3 Cover the mixture and chill.
4 Before serving, sprinkle with the coriander leaves.

## NARINCHI AGHTSAN
*Armenian orange salad*

This is a tangy salad of oranges and dates. It looks extremely decorative on a buffet table and is a refreshing accompaniment to any poultry dish.

*4 oranges*
*10 dates, stoned and chopped*
*1 tablespoon slivered almonds*
*1 tablespoon caster sugar*

*juice of 1 lemon*
*2½ fl oz (75ml) yoghurt*
*2½ fl oz (75ml) double cream*
*a pinch of cinnamon*

**1** Peel the oranges, removing as much of the white pith as possible.
**2** Slice them thinly crossways.
**3** Arrange the slices over a large platter.
**4** Scatter the chopped dates and the almonds over the oranges.
**5** In a small bowl mix together the sugar, lemon juice, yoghurt and cream.
**6** Pour this sauce over the salad, sprinkle with the cinnamon and serve.

## PORTAKAL SALATASI
*Orange and yoghurt salad*

This is an adaptation of an Ottoman salad popular throughout what was the Ottoman Empire. The use of *filfar* – an orange liqueur – or the Israeli liqueur *sabra* is optional, but if they are available do use them as they add a new and interesting flavour.

Try this salad with roast lamb or chicken.

*2 large oranges*
*1 small head lettuce*
*¼ head curly endive*
*3 tablespoons caster sugar*

*2 tablespoons* filfar *or* sabra *or*
  curaçao
*¼ pint (150ml) yoghurt*

**1** Peel the oranges and slice them very thinly crossways.
**2** Wash the lettuce leaves and endive, pat dry with kitchen paper and arrange in a salad bowl.
**3** Now arrange the orange slices decoratively around the centre of the bowl.

**4** Sprinkle the oranges with the sugar and liqueur and then place the salad in the refrigerator for at least 2 hours.

**5** When ready to serve beat the yoghurt until smooth and spoon it over the salad.

## SALADE SIB ZAMINI BA MAST
*Potato salad with yoghurt*

Most of the salads now popular in Iran are European in origin, although over the years they have been adapted to local tastes and ingredients. This salad is no exception. It is based on the Russian soured cream and potato salad.

*3–4 large potatoes*
*½ pint (300ml) yoghurt*
*¼ pint (150ml) soured cream (or use more yoghurt instead)*
*1 teaspoon salt*
*tablespoon fresh dill or 1 teaspoon dried dillweed*

*½ teaspoon black pepper*
*3 hard-boiled eggs, peeled and chopped*
*4 large dill pickles or ½ fresh cucumber, thinly sliced*
*fresh tarragon as a garnish (optional)*

**1** Cook the potatoes in a large pan of boiling water until tender.

**2** Allow to cool; peel and cut into small cubes.

**3** In a small bowl mix the yoghurt and soured cream together, then stir in the salt, black pepper and dill.

**4** Put the chopped potatoes, eggs and pickled or fresh cucumber into a large salad bowl.

**5** Pour the dressing over the top and then stir gently.

**6** Garnish and place in the refrigerator for at least 1 hour before serving.

### Variation

You can also try cubed cooked potatoes dressed with yoghurt mayonnaise (p. 168), horseradish sauce and herbs.

## PALAK RAETA
*Spinach with yoghurt and spices*

One of the splendid Indian *raetas*, or yoghurt-based salads; this dish makes an exciting use of spices. Serve chilled or at room temperature as an accompaniment to any curry or kebab.

| | |
|---|---|
| 1 lb (½kg) spinach, fresh or frozen | ½ teaspoon fenugreek seeds |
| 1 tablespoon ghee or vegetable oil | ½ teaspoon chilli powder |
| 1 teaspoon black mustard seeds | 1 teaspoon salt |
| 1 teaspoon cumin seeds | ½ pint (300ml) yoghurt |
| 1 teaspoon cumin powder | |

1  If using fresh spinach, wash thoroughly to remove all the grit and dirt. Place in a saucepan with sufficient boiling water to cover and simmer for about 10 minutes.

2  If using frozen spinach, thaw and simmer in boiling water for 5 to 10 minutes until tender.

3  Strain the spinach and squeeze out any remaining water.

4  Chop the spinach.

5  Heat the ghee or oil in a saucepan and fry the mustard seeds until they pop.

6  Add the cumin seeds and powder and the fenugreek, and continue to fry, stirring frequently.

7  When the fenugreek seeds turn a brownish colour remove the pan from the heat.

8  Stir in the chilli pepper and salt and allow to cool.

9  Add the yoghurt to the spice mixture and stir well.

10  Place the spinach in a serving bowl, pour the yoghurt over the top and stir well.


## WATERCRESS AND RADISH SALAD

I have found this salad with its cinnamon yoghurt dressing very successful with grilled fish and fish dishes generally.

> 1 cos lettuce
> 1 bunch watercress
> 12 radishes
> ½ pint (300ml) cinnamon yoghurt sauce (see p. 167)
> juice of ½ lemon

1 Remove any coarse lettuce leaves and wash the remaining ones carefully.

2 Trim and wash the watercress.

3 Pat the lettuce and watercress dry on kitchen paper.

4 Wash the radishes, trim and slice thinly.

5 Shred the lettuce leaves finely and place in a salad bowl.

6 Add the watercress and the radishes.

7 Pour the cinnamon yoghurt sauce over the salad, together with the lemon juice.

8 Toss well and chill for at least an hour before serving.

## SHOMINOV TZOO
### *Spinach and egg salad*

An unusual salad of fresh spinach and yoghurt combined to create a unique flavour. Serve with roast or grilled meat or poultry.

*½ lb (250g) fresh spinach leaves*
*4 spring onions, including green heads, finely sliced*
*½–¾ pint (300–450ml) yoghurt*
*2 fl oz (60ml) olive oil*
*1 teaspoon salt*
*½ teaspoon black pepper*
*4 hard-boiled eggs, shelled and chopped*
*about 15 black olives*
*pinch of paprika*

1 Wash the spinach leaves very thoroughly until all the sand and gravel have been removed.

2 Drain the leaves, pat dry with kitchen paper and then shred.

3 Mix the shredded leaves in a large salad bowl with the spring onions.

4 In a small bowl blend the yoghurt, olive oil, salt and pepper.

5 Stir in the chopped eggs.

6 Pour this mixture over the spinach and toss carefully so as not to break up the eggs too much.

7 Garnish with black olives and sprinkle paprika over the top.

8 Serve chilled.

## SALATA BI LABAN
*Arab mixed salad*

Popular in Egypt and Syria, this fresh, mixed salad receives extra flavour from the addition of yoghurt. It gives the vegetables a cool, tangy delicacy.

Serve with meat, poultry and kebab dishes.

| | |
|---|---|
| 1 green pepper, thinly sliced | juice of 1 lemon |
| 1 onion, finely sliced | 3 tablespoons olive oil |
| 4 tomatoes, sliced | 1 tablespoon chopped fresh mint or 1 |
| 1 clove garlic, crushed | teaspoon dried mint |
| 1 tablespoon finely chopped parsley | 1 teaspoon salt |
| 4–5 coriander seeds, crushed or ½ | a few grindings of black pepper |
| teaspoon coriander powder | ½ pint (300ml) yoghurt |

**1** Put the sliced pepper, onion and tomatoes into a large salad bowl together with all the other ingredients, apart from the yoghurt.

**2** Mix all the ingredients together and leave until ready to serve.

**3** Pour the yoghurt over the salad, mix and serve immediately.

## SURKI AGHTSAN
*Spiced dried yoghurt salad*

This is an Armenian salad from the mountains of Cilicia. It is one of the great classics of the region. I regard this as one of the most exciting and unusual salads I have ever tasted.

| | |
|---|---|
| 1 surki ball (see p. 21) | 1 small onion, thinly sliced |
| 4 tomatoes, thinly sliced | 2 tablespoons finely chopped parsley |
| 4 in (10cm) piece of cucumber, | 2 tablespoons olive oil |
| halved lengthways and thinly | juice of ½ lemon |
| sliced | |

**1** Break the *surki* ball into ½ in (1cm) pieces with a sharp knife.

**2** In a large bowl mix the sliced tomatoes, cucumber, onion and chopped parsley.

**3** Add the *surki* pieces, olive oil and lemon juice, and mix well.

**4** Serve on its own or as an accompaniment to any roast meat.

## ZEYTOV SURKI
### *Spiced dried yoghurt in oil*

A Cilician–Armenian salad dating from ancient times; simple
and tasty. It is excellent on its own with hot pitta bread or
*lavash* and *tan* – a yoghurt drink (see p. 174).

> 1 ball of surki *kept in olive oil (see p. 21)*
> 1 small onion, thinly sliced
> some black olives
> ½ teaspoon chilli pepper

1 Slice a ball of *surki* thinly.
2 Add the onion and toss gently.
3 Arrange on a plate and garnish with the olives and pepper.

## MAST-E-KHIAR
### *Labna with vegetables and nuts*

This slightly more elaborate version of *labna* is Iranian by
origin. It is one of those dishes that is sometimes eaten as an
appetizer, sometimes as a salad accompanying roast meats
and sometimes as a meal in itself.

*1 pint (600ml) yoghurt*
*1 cucumber, peeled and*
*  finely chopped*
*1 onion, grated*
*1 tablespoon finely chopped fresh*
*  mint or 1 teaspoon dried mint*
*2 oz (50g) walnuts, chopped*

*2 teaspoons salt*
*½ tablespoon fresh dill or ½*
*  teaspoon dried dillweed*
*2 oz (50g) currants*
*4 radishes, washed, trimmed and*
*  finely chopped*
*washed lettuce leaves as a garnish*

1 Use the yoghurt to prepare *labna* as described on p. 18.
2 Turn the *labna* into a mixing bowl and add all the remaining
ingredients except the radishes and lettuce leaves.
3 Mix the ingredients together.
4 Shape the mixture into small balls. If you have a melon scoop then
use that.
5 Arrange the lettuce leaves around a large plate, place the balls of
*mast-e-khiar* in the centre and sprinkle the chopped radishes over the
top.

## EGG AND YOGHURT SALAD

This simple egg salad can be a meal in its own right as well as making an excellent accompaniment to roast chicken or beef.

DRESSING
½ pint (300ml) yoghurt
1 teaspoon paprika
1 teaspoon sugar
1 tablespoon lemon juice
1 tablespoon orange juice
¼ teaspoon black pepper
1 tablespoon finely chopped parsley

SALAD
4 sticks celery, washed and finely sliced
4 hard-boiled eggs, peeled and sliced
2 carrots, peeled and grated
8 radishes, washed, trimmed and finely sliced
½ cucumber, sliced

**1** First prepare the dressing by combining all its ingredients in a large bowl.

**2** Set half the dressing aside and fold the celery through the remaining dressing.

**3** Spoon the celery into a salad bowl.

**4** Arrange the egg slices over the celery and then cover with grated carrot.

**5** Surround the edges of the bowl with the sliced radishes and cucumber.

**6** Spoon the remaining dressing over the top.

**7** Chill for about 30 minutes and serve.

## BISTAGOV-KHOZI AGHTSAN
### *Pistachio and ham salad*

This is a recipe of mine based on a traditional Armenian one of pistachios, soured cream and shredded chicken breasts. I find that chopped ham with salted pistachios gives more exciting results. *Haloumi* cheese can be bought from most continental shops. It is slightly salty.

SERVES SIX
6 oz (175g) haloumi *cheese (use Cheddar if you prefer)*
4 small eating apples
1 lb (½kg) cooked ham cut into small

½ in (1cm) pieces (or cooked breasts of chicken, shredded)
½ lb (250g) celery cut into ¼ in (½cm) slices

2 *spring onions, including green
    heads, cut into ¼ in (½cm) pieces*
6 *oz (175g) shelled pistachios*
1 *pint (600ml) yoghurt mayonnaise
    (see p. 168)*

*juice of 1 lemon*
1 *teaspoon salt*
½ *teaspoon cayenne pepper*
1 *teaspoon turmeric*

**1** Wash the cheese under cold running water to remove the brine and then cut into ½ in (1cm) cubes.

**2** Peel the apples, remove the cores and cut into ½ in (1cm) cubes.

**3** In a large bowl toss together the cheese, apples, ham, celery, spring onions and pistachios.

**4** Pour the yoghurt mayonnaise over the salad, together with the lemon juice, salt and cayenne pepper. Mix well.

**5** Allow to chill for an hour or so.

**6** Garnish with the turmeric and serve.

# VEGETABLE DISHES

### BAIGAN DAHI
*Aubergines with yoghurt*

An Indian dish which can be served as a snack with bread and fresh vegetables or as an accompaniment to curries and pilavs. Cheap, simple and tasty.

2 medium aubergines
3 tablespoons cooking oil
2 onions, finely chopped
3 cloves garlic, finely chopped
2 teaspoons finely grated fresh
  ginger
2 teaspoons ground coriander
1 teaspoon ground cumin

½ teaspoon turmeric
½ teaspoon chilli powder
1½ teaspoons salt
½ teaspoon garam masala
  (see p. 197)
sugar, optional
½ pint (300ml) yoghurt

**1** Place the aubergines under a hot grill or in a hot oven and cook until the flesh is soft throughout.

**2** Leave until cool enough to handle, peel and either chop the flesh finely or mash.

**3** Heat the oil in a saucepan and fry the onion, garlic and ginger until the onion is soft and golden.

**4** Add the coriander, cumin, turmeric and chilli powder and fry, stirring, for another minute.

**5** Stir in the salt and add the chopped or mashed aubergine.

**6** Stir and cook for a few minutes then sprinkle with the *garam masala*, cover and cook for 5 minutes longer.

**7** Taste and adjust seasoning if necessary. You can add a little sugar (about 2 teaspoons) here if you feel it is necessary.

**8** Beat the yoghurt until smooth and stir into the aubergines before serving.

## SISEROV LETSONADZ SUMPOOG
*Aubergines stuffed with chick peas*

This Armenian dish can be served as a starter or as a main course for vegetarians. A popular Lent dish.

½ lb (250g) chick peas, soaked
    overnight in cold water
4 medium aubergines
2 oz (50g) ghee or butter
1 onion, finely chopped
1 clove garlic, finely chopped
1 tablespoon tomato purée

1 teaspoon marjoram
1 teaspoon salt
½ teaspoon chilli powder
2 tablespoons chopped parsley
vegetable oil for frying
½ pint (300ml) yoghurt herb
    dressing (see p. 170)

1  Rinse the chick peas under cold running water.

2  Place them in a large saucepan threequarters filled with water and bring to the boil. Spoon off any scum that comes to the surface.

3  Reduce heat and simmer vigorously for about 1 hour or until the chick peas are tender. It may be necessary to add more boiling water.

4  Strain into a colander, rinse under cold water and set aside until cool enough to handle.

5  Meanwhile cut the heads off the aubergines and remove most of the flesh and seeds inside with an apple corer without damaging the shells.

6  Bring a large pan half filled with water to the boil, add the aubergines and simmer for 10 minutes.

7  Drain the vegetables and set aside.

8  Meanwhile, by pressing each chick pea between thumb and forefinger, remove its skin and discard.

9  Melt the butter in a large frying pan, add the onion and garlic and sauté until golden brown.

10  Stir in the tomato purée, marjoram, salt, chilli powder, chick peas and 1 tablespoon of the parsley.

11  Cook for a few minutes and then set aside.

12  Fill the cavity of each aubergine with the chick pea mixture.

13  Pour about ¼ pint (150ml) vegetable oil into a large frying pan and heat.

14  Add the aubergines and fry gently for 10 to 15 minutes, turning carefully from time to time, until cooked all over.

15  Serve sprinkled with the remaining parsley and accompanied by the yoghurt herb dressing.

## KHARAPAKHI LOBI MADZNOV
*Green beans with yoghurt sauce*

This is traditionally made with soured cream and tomatoes. I give a simpler version using only yoghurt. Serve it with meat or poultry dishes, or on its own with bread and pickles.

*1 lb (½kg) French beans, trimmed and halved crossways*
*2 oz (50g) butter*
*1 onion, finely chopped*
*1 green pepper, seeds and white pith removed and discarded, sliced thinly*

*1 tablespoon chopped fresh basil or 1 teaspoon dried basil*
*¾ pint (450ml) garlic yoghurt sauce (see p. 167)*
*1 tablespoon finely chopped parsley*

**1** Bring a large pan, half filled with lightly salted water, to the boil.
**2** Add the beans and boil for about 10 minutes or until they are tender but still firm.
**3** Drain and set aside.
**4** Melt the butter in a large frying pan, add the onion and green pepper and sauté until soft.
**5** Stir in the beans and basil and simmer for a further 5 minutes.
**6** Spoon the mixture into a serving dish, pour the garlic yoghurt sauce over the top and sprinkle with the parsley.

## BEETROOT WITH YOGHURT SAUCE

An Arab dish that makes a good accompaniment to roast chicken and grilled fish.

*1 oz (25g) butter*
*2 oz (50g) flour*
*½ pint (300ml) chicken stock*
*1 small onion, finely chopped*
*½ teaspoon dried dillweed*
*½ teaspoon salt*

*¼ teaspoon white pepper*
*¼ pint (150ml) yoghurt*
*6 medium-sized beetroots, cooked, peeled and sliced*
*1 tablespoon chopped parsley*

**1** Melt the butter in a saucepan.
**2** Stir in the flour and cook for 1 minute.
**3** Remove the pan from the heat and slowly pour in the stock, stirring constantly.

**4** When the sauce is smooth return the pan to the heat.

**5** Stirring continuously, bring the sauce to the boil and cook for 5 minutes or until the sauce has thickened.

**6** Add the onion, dill, salt and pepper, and cook for 5 to 10 minutes until the onion is soft.

**7** Put the yoghurt into a small bowl and stir in 2 tablespoons of the hot sauce.

**8** Now pour the mixture back into the sauce.

**9** Gently mix in the beetroot slices. Make sure that all the slices are covered with the sauce.

**10** Leave over a very low heat for 2 to 3 minutes to heat through but do not boil.

**11** Pour the beetroot and sauce into a serving dish, sprinkle with chopped parsley and serve hot.

## BRUSSELS SPROUTS IN YOGHURT

I like this vegetable dish very much. It is one of Irfan Orga's (from *Cooking with Yogurt*) and is a most original accompaniment to any roast meat.

2 lb (1kg) brussels sprouts,
  rough outer leaves removed and
  a slit made in the base of each
  stalk
½ oz (15g) butter
2 large tomatoes, blanched, skinned
  and chopped

2 teaspoons chopped fresh chives or
  1 teaspoon dried chives
salt and pepper to taste
¼ teaspoon ground nutmeg
½ pint (300ml) yoghurt, stabilized
1 oz (25g) grated Parmesan cheese
1 oz (25g) toasted, slivered almonds

**1** Bring a large saucepan half filled with slightly salted water to the boil.

**2** Add the sprouts and simmer until they are just tender.

**3** Drain in a colander.

**4** Butter a casserole dish and empty the sprouts into it.

**5** Arrange the chopped tomatoes over the top and then sprinkle with the chives.

**6** Season with the salt, pepper and nutmeg.

**7** Beat the yoghurt until smooth and pour over the vegetables.

**8** Sprinkle with the cheese and bake in an oven preheated to 350°F (180°C, gas 4) for about 20 minutes or until golden brown.

**9** Scatter the toasted almonds over the top and serve.

## BOILED CABBAGE WITH YOGHURT

Traditionally this Hungarian/Romanian vegetable dish is made with soured cream. I have substituted yoghurt and it is delicious. It is usually served with roast pork, but goes well with lamb and beef as well.

| | |
|---|---|
| *1 firm white cabbage (2–3 lb, 1–1½kg)* | *1 teaspoon dried mint or 1 tablespoon chopped fresh mint* |
| *2 oz (50g) butter* | *½ pint (300ml) yoghurt* |
| *1 small onion, finely chopped* | *1 clove garlic, crushed* |
| *2 teaspoons salt* | *a few grindings of black pepper* |
| *1 teaspoon caraway seeds* | |

**1** Remove the coarse outer leaves of the cabbage, then cut it into quarters and remove the central hard core.

**2** Cut the cabbage into narrow strips, wash and drain.

**3** Melt the butter in a large saucepan and sauté the onion until it is soft but not brown.

**4** Add the chopped cabbage together with the salt, caraway seeds, mint and just sufficient water to prevent the cabbage sticking while cooking.

**5** Simmer until the cabbage is just tender, stirring occasionally.

**6** Pour the yoghurt into a small bowl and whisk in the garlic.

**7** Pour this mixture over the cabbage, stir and heat through but do not boil.

**8** Turn into a serving dish, sprinkle with black pepper and serve.

## YOGOURTLU HAVUÇ SALATASI
### *Fried carrots in yoghurt*

This is a popular Turkish and Balkan dish that goes well with grilled and roasted lamb or beef.

1 lb (½kg) carrots, peeled or scraped
   and washed
2 tablespoons flour
3 tablespoons olive oil
1 teaspoon salt
½ teaspoon ground white pepper
½ teaspoon caraway seeds
½ pint (300ml) yoghurt
1 tablespoon chopped fresh mint or 1
   teaspoon dried mint

**1** Cut carrots crossways into ¼ in (½cm) slices.

**2** Cook in boiling salted water for 10 to 15 minutes or until tender.

**3** Drain and dry thoroughly on kitchen paper.

**4** Toss the carrots in the flour.

**5** Heat the oil in a large frying pan, add the floured carrots and cook, turning occasionally, until browned on both sides.

**6** Add the salt, pepper and caraway seeds and stir well.

**7** Warm the yoghurt through in a small saucepan but do not boil.

**8** Arrange the carrots on a large plate and pour over any of the oil left in the pan.

**9** Pour the yoghurt over the top, sprinkle with the mint and serve immediately.

## TZVOV TUTMIG
### *Fried courgettes in yoghurt*

Yoghurt has a great affinity with fried vegetables. You can use aubergines, mushrooms or tomatoes instead of courgettes.

4 large courgettes
1–2 cloves garlic, crushed
1 teaspoon salt
1 teaspoon dried dillweed
1 teaspoon dried mint
2 eggs
vegetable oil for frying
½ pint (300ml) yoghurt
1 tablespoon finely chopped parsley

**1** Wash the courgettes, remove heads and tails and cut into ¼ in (½cm) slices.

**2** Half fill a saucepan with slightly salted water and bring to the boil.

**3** Add the courgette slices and cook until just tender.

**4** Strain into a colander.

**5** Break the eggs into a bowl, add the garlic, salt, dill and mint and beat with a fork.

**6** Heat a little of the oil in a large frying pan.

**7** Dip some of the courgette slices in the egg and place in the pan.

**8** Fry on both sides until golden.

**9** Remove to a serving dish and keep warm while you cook the remaining slices in the same way.

**10** Pour the yoghurt over the top and sprinkle with the parsley.

**11** Serve warm with roast meats or cold as an appetizer.


## BRASS AGHTSAN
### *Leeks with yoghurt sauce*

A delightfully and delicately flavoured accompaniment to fish or chicken dishes.

*8 leeks*
*juice of 1 lemon*
*10 or more peppercorns*
*1 teaspoon salt*
*4 coriander seeds*
*3 sprigs of parsley*

*3 spring onions, finely chopped, including green heads*
*1 pint (½l) yoghurt mustard sauce (see p. 171)*
*2 tablespoons chopped parsley as a garnish*

**1** Cut off the roots and most of the green tops of the leeks and remove any coarse outer leaves.

**2** Wash carefully under cold running water to remove all the grit and sand between the layers.

**3** Prepare a stock by bringing 1 pint (½l) of water to the boil in a saucepan.

**4** Add to the pan the lemon juice, peppercorns, salt, coriander seeds, parsley sprigs and chopped onions and simmer for about 10 minutes.

**5** Arrange the leeks in a large frying pan or flameproof dish and pour the stock over the top.

**6** Cover and simmer gently for 20 to 30 minutes or until the leeks are tender.

**7** Switch off the heat and leave to cool.

**8** Remove the leeks and drain on kitchen paper.

**9** Arrange the leeks on a large plate and pour the yoghurt mustard sauce over the top.

**10** Sprinkle with the chopped parsley and serve.

## VOSPOV TUTUM
### *Lentils with pumpkin*

Great recipes are often made with the simplest ingredients and nothing could be simpler than lentils or pumpkin.
Serve with meat dishes, stews, and grills.

*3 oz (75g) whole brown lentils*
*1½ lb (¾kg) peeled pumpkin*
*2 oz (50g) butter*
*1 onion, finely chopped*

*1 oz (25g) sugar*
*½ teaspoon salt*
*3 tablespoons finely chopped parsley*
*½ pint (300ml) yoghurt*

1 Soak the lentils for a few hours in cold water and then rinse under cold running water.

2 Place the lentils in a saucepan and add sufficient water to cover by at least 1 in (3cm).

3 Bring to the boil and simmer for about 30 minutes or until the lentils are tender, adding more water if necessary. Drain and set aside.

4 Meanwhile cut the pumpkin flesh into slices 2 ins (5cm) long and ½ in (1cm) thick.

5 Put the pumpkin pieces into a large saucepan and add enough water to cover by 1 in (3cm).

6 Bring to the boil and simmer until the pumpkin is just tender. It will go mushy if overcooked.

7 Drain the pumpkin and set aside.

8 Melt the butter in a deep pan, add the onion and sauté until it is golden brown.

9 Add the lentils and pumpkin, and sprinkle the sugar and salt over the top.

10 Mix them together gently, taking care not to break up the pumpkin.

11 Simmer for 3 to 5 minutes.

12 Pour the vegetables into a large serving dish and sprinkle with the parsley.

13 Serve with the yoghurt on the side; 2–3 tablespoons stirred into each portion of vegetables will suffice.

## BORANI YE GHARCH
*Yoghurt with mushrooms*

A Persian dish that can be eaten as an appetizer with salad and pitta bread or as an accompaniment to any roast or grilled meat and to pastry dishes.

| | |
|---|---|
| *1 lb (½kg) mushrooms* | *¾ pint (450ml) yoghurt* |
| *2 oz (50g) butter* | *1 teaspoon salt* |
| *8 fl oz (250ml) chicken stock* | *1 clove garlic, very finely chopped* |

**1** Wash the mushrooms and pat dry on kitchen paper.
**2** Slice the mushrooms.
**3** Melt the butter in a saucepan and sauté the mushrooms for a few minutes.
**4** Add the stock and simmer for 15 to 20 minutes until most of the liquid has evaporated.
**5** Remove from the heat, drain the mushrooms and leave to cool for a few minutes.
**6** Add the yoghurt and salt and stir well.
**7** Sprinkle the garlic over the top.
**8** Serve warm.

## HUNGARIAN MUSHROOMS IN YOGHURT

This is a tasty mushroom dish which is an excellent accompaniment to any meat dish, either hot or cold.

| | |
|---|---|
| *¾ lb (350g) mushrooms* | *¾ teaspoon salt* |
| *2 oz (50g) butter* | *½ teaspoon black pepper* |
| *1 onion, finely sliced* | *½ teaspoon paprika* |
| *1 green pepper, finely sliced* | *¼ pint (150ml) yoghurt blended* |
| *1 tablespoon finely chopped parsley* | *with 1 level tablespoon plain flour* |

**1** Remove the stalks from the mushrooms, then wipe the caps and slice thinly.
**2** Melt the butter in a large saucepan and fry the onion and green pepper until the onion slices are golden brown.
**3** Add the mushrooms, ⅓ pint (200ml) water, parsley, salt, black pepper and paprika.

**4** Stew the vegetables, stirring occasionally, until the water has evaporated.

**5** When the water has evaporated add the stabilized yoghurt and heat through, but do not boil.

**6** Serve immediately.

## SAUTÉED PARSNIPS

A simple side dish which goes well with most roast meat and fish dishes.

*2 lb (1kg) parsnips*
*2 oz (50g) butter*
*1 small onion, finely chopped*
*salt to taste*

*½ pint (300ml) yoghurt mustard*
*sauce (see p. 171)*
*1 tablespoon chopped parsley*

**1** Cut the tops and roots off the parsnips, then scrape and wash them.

**2** Cut each one in half lengthways and remove the hard core.

**3** Half fill a large saucepan with lightly salted water, add the parsnips and boil for 20 minutes.

**4** Drain and pat dry on kitchen paper.

**5** Melt the butter in a large saucepan or frying pan, add the onion and sauté for a few minutes.

**6** Add the parsnips and fry gently for 8 to 10 minutes, turning occasionally. Salt.

**7** Arrange the vegetables on a large plate and pour the yoghurt mustard sauce over the top.

**8** Sprinkle with the chopped parsley and serve warm.

## MATAR PANIR
### Peas with cream cheese

This is not strictly a yoghurt dish, but I justify its inclusion on three grounds. First because it is made of *panir* – a cream cheese the recipe for which I have included on p. 19. Secondly, because it can also be made with *labna* (the Arab version of cream cheese) or with *chortan* (the Armenian dried yoghurt) (pp. 18 and 20). And now the most important reason – because I like it.

If you possibly can, make your own *panir* or *labna* and trap the whey, as you need it for this recipe. If you prefer to buy the cheese try fresh *pecorino*.

*8 oz (250g)* panir *or* labna *– made*
*from 2 pints (1l) yoghurt –*
*together with its whey (If using*
pecorino *then make up ¼ pint*
*(150ml) skimmed milk.)*
*4 oz (125g) ghee or butter*
*½ teaspoon salt*
*2 onions, finely sliced*

*6 oz (175g) fresh or frozen peas*
*½ teaspoon paprika*
*½ teaspoon ground ginger*
*½ teaspoon* garam masala
*(see p. 197)*
*1 tablespoon finely chopped*
*coriander or mint leaves*

1 Cut the cheese into ½ in (1cm) cubes.

2 Melt the ghee or butter in a saucepan, add the cubes of cheese and fry until they are a light brown.

3 Mix the whey or skimmed milk with the salt in a bowl.

4 With a slotted spoon remove the cheese cubes from the fat and place in the whey or milk to soak for about 15 minutes.

5 Meanwhile fry the onions in the same fat until they are golden brown.

6 Remove the onions and set aside.

7 Put ¼ pint (150ml) water and the peas into the saucepan, bring to the boil and simmer until the peas are just tender.

8 Drain off the liquid leaving the peas in the pan.

9 Return the onions and cheese to the pan together with the paprika and ginger and stir gently over a very low heat for 2 to 3 minutes.

10 Finally add the *garam masala* and stir gently for a further 2 minutes.

11 Turn into a serving dish, sprinkle with the coriander or mint leaves and serve immediately.

### YOGURTLU PATATES
*Potatoes with yoghurt and chives*

A popular Balkan and Turkish speciality. The addition of whipped egg whites almost makes this a soufflé. It goes extremely well with all forms of roast meat.

2 lb (1kg) potatoes, peeled, boiled in
   lightly salted water and drained
4 tablespoons yoghurt
1 tablespoon butter
2 eggs, separated

1 tablespoon chopped chives
½ teaspoon thyme
¼ teaspoon paprika
salt and pepper to taste
a pinch of nutmeg

1  Mash the potatoes with the yoghurt and butter until smooth.

2  Beat in the egg yolks, chives, thyme, paprika, salt and pepper.

3  Lightly butter a soufflé dish.

4  Whisk the egg whites until stiff and gently fold into the potato mixture.

5  Spoon the mixture into the soufflé dish, smooth the surface and sprinkle with nutmeg.

6  Place in an oven preheated to 350°F (180°C, gas 4) and cook for 25 to 30 minutes.

7  Serve immediately.

## PAKORHAS
### *Vegetable and yoghurt fritters*

*Pakorhas* are traditionally vegetable savouries but you can use fruits as well. The most popular *pakorhas* are *baigan pakorha* (aubergine), *saag pakorha* (spinach) and *praza pakorha* (onion). The two latter are found on the menus of most good Indian restaurants.

   The art of successful *pakorhas* is in the batter, which is made with *sieve besan* – chick-pea flour obtainable from most Indian shops. The recipe below is for *praza pakorhas* – onion *pakorhas*.

½ teaspoon chilli powder
½ teaspoon turmeric
1 teaspoon salt
1 teaspoon garam masala
   (see p. 197)
6 oz (175g) sieve besan

1 pint (600ml) yoghurt
1 clove garlic, crushed
2 onions
¼–½ pint (150–300ml) vegetable
   oil for frying

1  Sieve the chilli powder, turmeric, salt, *garam masala* and *sieve besan* into a bowl.

2  Put the yoghurt and garlic into a large mixing bowl and whisk until smooth.

**3** Sifting the dry mixture again, add it a little at a time to the yoghurt, stirring continuously, preferrably with a wire whisk.

**4** Keep whisking until you have a smooth batter which forms small peaks which disintegrate after 15 to 20 seconds. You may find that you need a little more or less flour depending on how liquid the yoghurt is.

**5** Leave the batter to stand for 30 minutes and then whisk once more.

**6** Meanwhile peel the onions and slice crossways to form onion rings.

**7** Heat the oil in a large pan.

**8** Dip each onion ring into the batter and fry individually in the fat until pale golden on both sides.

**9** Lift out with a slotted spoon and drain on kitchen paper.

**10** Repeat with the remaining rings.

**11** If you like the *pakorhas* very crisp then, just before serving, return to the hot fat for about 20 seconds and drain and serve immediately.

### Baigan pakorhas

Aubergines make excellent fritters. If you make them, bear in mind the following points:

1 Slice the aubergines ⅛ in (25mm) thick crossways.

2 Make sure that the oil is not too hot, or the fat and *pakorhas* will become a dirty brown – and not too cool, or they will become laden with excess fat.

NOTE The batter will keep for weeks if covered and left in the refrigerator. This makes it very useful if you want hors d'oeuvre or teatime snacks in a hurry.

### ARSHDA MADZNOV
*Armenian macaroni moussaka*

This dish can be a starter or a main course. It is an excellent vegetarian dish; it can also be served as an accompaniment to grilled or roast meat. You can use spaghetti instead of macaroni and you can also add either sliced mushrooms or sliced green peppers or both.

*1 large or 2 medium aubergines*
*8 oz (250g) cooked macaroni cut into*
  *1 in (3cm) pieces*
*2 or 3 tomatoes, thinly sliced*
*½ pint (300ml) yoghurt stabilized*
  *with 1 tablespoon of flour*

*½ pint (300ml) chicken stock*
*1 teaspoon salt*
*½ teaspoon black pepper*
*3 oz (75g) grated cheese – Cheddar,*
  *Gruyère or* feta
*1 oz (25g) chopped almonds*

**1** Cut the stem and bottom from each aubergine, then wash and cut lengthwise into ¾ in (2cm) pieces.

**2** Put the slices on a large plate, sprinkle with salt and set aside for 30 minutes.

**3** Put the macaroni in a well-buttered casserole.

**4** Wash the aubergine slices and pat dry.

**5** Cover the macaroni first with the tomato slices and then with the aubergine slices.

**6** Mix the yoghurt and chicken stock together; season and spoon over the aubergines.

**7** Mix the cheese and almonds together and sprinkle over the top of the casserole.

**8** Preheat oven to 350°F (180°C, gas 4) and bake for about an hour or until the top is golden brown.


## PATATES ME YAOURTI
### Stuffed potatoes

This is a simple, wholesome dish of Balkan origin. It makes a tasty snack lunch served with a fresh salad. If possible use *feta* cheese, obtainable from most Middle Eastern stores; otherwise any white cheese will do.

*4 large potatoes*
*a little melted butter*
*2 oz (50g) grated* feta *or white*
  *cheese*
*2 oz (50g) cooked minced meat (lamb*
  *or beef)*

*2 tablespoons chopped chives*
*¼ pint (150ml) yoghurt*
*1 teaspoon salt*
*½ teaspoon black pepper*
*a pinch of nutmeg*

1 Wash and dry the potatoes.

2 Brush the potatoes with the melted butter and place in a lightly buttered ovenproof dish.

3 Cook in an oven preheated to 400°F (200°C, gas 6) for about 1 hour.

4 Remove from the oven and leave until cool enough to handle.

5 Remove a small slice from the top of each potato.

6 Using a small spoon, scoop out as much of the insides as possible and place in a mixing bowl. Take care not to break the potato shells.

7 Add the cheese, meat, chives, yoghurt, salt and pepper to the potato pieces and mix the ingredients together.

8 Pile the mixture into the potato shells.

9 Place any remaining filling in a small saucepan.

10 Rearrange the potatoes in the casserole, place a dab of butter on each and cook in a very hot oven (450°F, 230°C, gas 7) for about 10 minutes.

11 Meanwhile heat any remaining filling through, but do not burn.

12 Place the extra filling in the middle of a large plate and arrange the potatoes around it.

13 Sprinkle with the nutmeg and serve immediately.

## PANCHAREGHENI PORANI
### *Armenian vegetable stew*

This vegetarian dish can be eaten either as a main dish or as an accompaniment to roast meat. Serve with roast potatoes or a plain rice pilav. A simple, wholesome and economical dish.

| | |
|---|---|
| *3 medium aubergines* | *1 clove garlic, crushed* |
| *3 courgettes* | *1 teaspoon black pepper* |
| *salt* | *2 eggs* |
| *4 oz (100g) French beans* | *½ pint (300ml) garlic yoghurt sauce* |
| *4 oz (100g) butter* | *(see p. 167)* |
| *1 green or red pepper, sliced* | *a pinch of paprika for garnish* |

1 Remove the stems and tails of the aubergines and courgettes.

2 Cut them into ¼ in (½cm) slices crossways.

3 Arrange the slices on a large plate, sprinkle with salt and leave for 30 minutes.

**4** Meanwhile wash, top and tail the French beans and cut into 2 in (5cm) pieces.

**5** Put the beans in a pan of boiling, lightly salted water and cook for 5 to 10 minutes.

**6** Drain and dry with kitchen paper.

**7** Drain, rinse and dry the aubergine and courgette slices.

**8** Melt the butter in a large saucepan or casserole, add the aubergines and courgettes and fry, stirring occasionally, for about 10 minutes.

**9** Add the beans, green pepper, garlic, pepper, and 2 teaspoons salt.

**10** Stir, cover and simmer until all the vegetables are just cooked – probably 20 to 30 minutes. Stir occasionally.

**11** Break the eggs into a bowl, beat with a fork and stir into the vegetables.

**12** As soon as the egg is cooked remove from the heat.

**13** Empty into a serving dish, spoon the garlic yoghurt sauce over it and sprinkle with the paprika.


## GAGHAMPI PATOUG
### *Cabbage leaves stuffed with meat*

Stuffed cabbage – with or without meat – is popular in Turkey and Armenia. Armenians add garlic yoghurt sauce to the stuffed leaves. Yoghurt and *burghul* have a great affinity for one another.

*2–3 lb (1–1½ kg) white cabbage*
*vinegar*
*4 oz (100g) prunes*
*4 oz (100g) dried apricots*
*1 small onion, sliced*
*2 tablespoons tomato purée*
*stock or water*
*salt and pepper*

*1 tablespoon chopped parsley*
*4 oz (100g) rice or coarse* burghul,
*washed thoroughly*
*1 teaspoon sweet basil*
*1 teaspoon allspice*
*1 teaspoon black pepper*
*2 teaspoons salt*
*4 oz (100g) chopped walnuts*

**FILLING**
*1 lb (½kg) minced lamb*
*1 large onion, finely chopped*

**TO SERVE**
*1 pint (½l) garlic yoghurt sauce*
*(see p. 167)*

**1** Put all the ingredients for the filling into a large bowl and knead well, adding about ¼ pint (150ml) cold water.

**2** Cut the cabbage in half and gently separate the leaves.

**3** Drop them into boiling water and cook gently for about 10 minutes until soft.

**4** Drain and sprinkle with a little vinegar.

**5** When cool cut through the thickest part of the central vein so that the leaves lie flat.

**6** Taking one leaf at a time put a tablespoon of meat mixture in the centre and wrap in the same way as described in *derevi patoug*, p. 94.

**7** Lay any broken leaves in the base of a large saucepan to prevent burning and arrange the rolls in the pan with the dried fruit and onion slices between the layers.

**8** Dilute the tomato purée in a bowl with sufficient stock or water to cover the rolls.

**9** Season to taste.

**10** Cook for approximately 1 hour or until the leaves are tender and the filling cooked.

**11** Serve immediately, accompanied by the garlic yoghurt sauce.

## SHEIKH-EL-MAHSHI BI LABAN
*Stuffed courgettes in a yoghurt sauce*

This is one of the most popular dishes from Aleppo, Syria, which is famed for its rich and spicy cuisine. A good accompaniment is a rice pilav.

2 tablespoons ghee or unsalted
  butter, the best substitute for the
  hamma *used in Syria*
1 onion, finely chopped
1 lb (½kg) minced meat, lamb or
  beef
1½ teaspoons salt
½ teaspoon black pepper
1 teaspoon allspice

2 oz (50g) pine kernels – if
  unavailable use coarsely chopped
  walnuts
12 medium-sized courgettes
1 pint (½l) yoghurt stabilized with 2
  eggs
1 oz (25g) butter
1 clove garlic, crushed
1 teaspoon dried mint

**1** Heat the fat in a large frying pan, add the onion and sauté until soft and transparent.

**2** Add the meat and fry, stirring frequently, over a fairly high heat until the meat is dark brown.

**3** Lower the heat and stir in the salt, pepper, allspice and pine kernels.

**4** Add a few tablespoons of water, cover and simmer for at least 30 minutes or until the meat is very tender.

**5** Meanwhile prepare the courgettes by first slicing off the stalk ends.

**6** Remove as much of the flesh as possible with an apple corer. Ideally the vegetable shell should be about ¼ in (½cm) thick. Take care not to split or make holes in the shells.

**7** Fill each courgette with the meat mixture.

**8** Arrange the courgettes in a large saucepan and place a plate over the top to hold them in place.

**9** Add sufficient lightly salted water to cover, bring to the boil and then lower the heat and simmer until the vegetables are tender.

**10** Pour the stabilized yoghurt into a small bowl and stir in a few tablespoons of the hot stock.

**11** Remove the saucepan from the heat and remove the plate.

**12** Add the yoghurt slowly to the pan, return to the heat and simmer over a very low heat.

**13** Melt the butter in a small pan, add the garlic and mint, fry for a few minutes and pour into the saucepan.

**14** Taste and season with a little more salt if necessary.

**15** Serve immediately.

## YOGURTLU BIBER DOLMACI
### *Green peppers stuffed with meat and yoghurt*

This is an unusual variation of a dish popular throughout the Middle East. The peppers in this recipe are stuffed with meat, nuts, breadcrumbs and yoghurt. Serve them hot with rice and salad as a main meal or warm as an appetizer.

*4 large green peppers*
*2 oz (50g) ghee or butter*
*1 onion, finely chopped*
*1 oz (25g) mushrooms, thinly sliced*

*8 oz (225g) minced meat – lamb is*
*   the traditional choice, but beef is*
*   perfectly acceptable*
*1 teaspoon salt*

½ teaspoon black pepper
1 oz (25g) breadcrumbs
1 tablespoon chopped parsley
2 tablespoons pine kernels, if you

can find them and afford them –
otherwise use walnuts
8 fl oz (250ml) yoghurt

**1** Cut a thin slice from the stalk end of each pepper. Retain the stalks.

**2** Remove the seeds and white pith.

**3** Half fill a large saucepan with lightly salted water and bring to the boil.

**4** Add the peppers, cook for 4 to 5 minutes, drain and leave to cool.

**5** Meanwhile melt the ghee or butter in a saucepan and sauté the onion and mushrooms until soft.

**6** Add the meat and cook for about 15 minutes, stirring frequently.

**7** Season with the salt and pepper and remove from the heat.

**8** Place the breadcrumbs, parsley, pine kernels or walnuts, the meat mixture and the yoghurt in a large bowl and mix well together.

**9** Fill the peppers with this mixture. Press the filling down tightly and replace the tops.

**10** Standing the peppers upright, fit them tightly into an ovenproof dish.

**11** Add about 1 in (3cm) water and bake in an oven preheated to 375°F (190°C, gas 5) for 30 to 45 minutes.

## DEREVI PATOUG
### Stuffed vine leaves

Stuffed vegetables and fruit are a traditional part of Middle Eastern cuisine. Whereas Arabs, Turks and Greeks use rice, Armenians prefer to use *burghul*, and usually serve a yoghurt sauce with the vegetables. In this version the leaves are wrapped around a filling of meat and spices. If a vine is available then pick the leaves in late May or early June when they are at their tenderest.

*1 lb (½kg) vine leaves, fresh or
  preserved*

**FILLING**
*1 lb (½kg) minced lamb
1 onion, finely chopped
1 green pepper, chopped
2 tablespoons chopped parsley
6 oz (175g) coarse* burghul
*2 tomatoes, blanched, skinned and
  chopped
2 tablespoons chopped fresh herbs
  e.g. coriander, mint, basil,
  marjoram
2 oz (50g) pine kernels or roughly
  chopped walnuts*

*2 teaspoons salt
1 teaspoon black pepper
1 teaspoon allspice*

**SAUCE**
*sufficient stock or water to cover the
  leaves
2 tablespoons tomato purée
2 cloves garlic, crushed
juice of 1 lemon
salt and pepper to taste*

**TO SERVE**
*1 pt (600ml) garlic yoghurt sauce
  (see p. 167)*

**1** If you are using fresh vine leaves, pick new and tender ones. If using preserved ones kept in brine, rinse under cold running water first.

**2** Immerse the fresh leaves in boiling salted water in a saucepan and boil for 2 to 3 minutes. Pour off the water and spread out the leaves on kitchen paper to drain.

**3** Put all the filling ingredients in a large bowl and knead until the mixture is well blended and smooth.

**4** To fill the vine leaves: first lay one leaf out flat, smooth side down and veins uppermost.

**5** Cut off the stalk. Arrange a small ridge of filling across the centre at the widest part of the leaf. Fold the bottom of the leaf up over the filling. Fold the sides over towards the centre. Roll up towards the tip of the leaf.

**6** You will now have a small cigar-shaped parcel.

**7** Repeat until the leaves and filling are used up.

**8** Use any remaining broken leaves to line the bottom of a medium to large saucepan – this helps to prevent burning.

**9** Pack the stuffed vine leaves carefully and tightly in layers.

**10** Place a large plate, bottom side up, over the leaves covering as many as possible, and hold it down with a small weight. This will prevent the leaves moving around while cooking and so coming undone.

**11** Mix all the sauce ingredients together and pour into the saucepan.

**12** Bring to the boil and then simmer for about 1 hour or until the stuffing is cooked and the leaves tender. It may be necessary to add a little more water.

**13** Arrange the vine leaves on a large platter and serve with the garlic yoghurt sauce. It is normally poured over the stuffed leaves.

**14** Reserve any remaining stock and use it to reheat any stuffed leaves not consumed immediately.

# EGG DISHES

### TZVADZEGH
*Omelette*

Yoghurt can be used extensively as an accompaniment to all kinds of omelettes. Serve it plain, with garlic or with herbs.

I have chosen a few recipes to show the possibilities. Experiment to your heart's content.

SERVES ONE
2 eggs
¼ teaspoon paprika
salt to taste

1 oz (25g) butter
1 teaspoon chopped parsley
¼ pint (150g) plain yoghurt or
    garlic yoghurt sauce (see p. 167)

1 Break the eggs into a small bowl, add the paprika and salt and whisk with a fork.
2 Melt the butter in a small frying pan.
3 Pour the egg mixture into the pan, stir with the fork and cook over a medium heat.
4 When the omelette is just set, sprinkle the parsley over the top, fold in half and slide on to a plate.
5 Serve either with plain yoghurt or with a garlic yoghurt sauce.

### Basturma or yershig omelette

Two of my favourite omelettes require ingredients which are, unfortunately, rather difficult to track down. You may find them in Greek, Armenian or other Middle Eastern shops. They are: *basturma* – raw dried beef which is salted, covered with a mixture of spices, including fenugreek, and then hung up to dry in a cool place for days; and *yershig* – minced meat sausage highly spiced with garlic, chilli and other spices. If you cannot find this then you could use a garlic-seasoned sausage instead.

**1** Fry the *basturma* or *yershig* in the butter and then proceed as with the plain omelette.

### Bargoog chor tzvadzegh

A recipe from the Erzenjan, eastern Turkey.

*3 dried apricots, quartered*

**1** Fry the apricots for a few minutes in butter, then proceed as for the plain omelette.

## ENGUIZI MISSOV TZVADZEGH
### *Omelette with meat and walnuts*

This is a typical Armenian omelette, especially popular in the winter months. It is often eaten as a snack with *lavash* or pitta bread. However, with fried potatoes and a bowl of salad it makes an inexpensive main meal.

*2 oz (50g) ghee or butter*
*1 lb (½kg) minced beef or lamb*
*1 onion, finely chopped*
*4 oz (100g) walnuts, coarsely chopped*
*1 teaspoon salt*
*½ teaspoon black pepper*

*½ teaspoon ground cumin*
*8 eggs*
*½ pint (300ml) garlic yoghurt sauce (see p. 167)*
*1 teaspoon paprika*
*tomato slices, radishes and spring onions for garnish*

**1** Melt the ghee or butter in a large frying pan, add the minced meat and fry, stirring frequently, until the meat is lightly browned.

**2** Add the chopped onion and fry for a few more minutes.

**3** Now add the walnuts, salt, black pepper and cumin, and fry for 15–20 minutes, stirring frequently.

**4** Break the eggs into a bowl and beat with a fork.

**5** Pour the eggs into the pan and fry gently until the eggs are set.

**6** Slide the omelette on to a plate, pour the garlic yoghurt sauce over the top, sprinkle with the paprika and serve at once with the garnishes.

## PASHA'S OMELETTE

This is my adaptation of a Turkish omelette. I have added mushrooms and tomatoes to give it extra flavour and colour.

1 oz (25g) butter
1 onion, finely chopped
6 button mushrooms, wiped clean
   and thinly sliced
2 tomatoes, finely chopped
8 eggs

3 tablespoons grated Parmesan
   cheese
¼ pint (150ml) yoghurt
1 clove garlic, crushed
½ teaspoon cumin
½ teaspoon paprika

1 In a shallow ovenproof dish melt the butter over a moderate heat and sauté the onion until soft.

2 Add the mushrooms and tomatoes and cook until soft.

3 Beat the eggs and pour over the vegetables.

4 Sprinkle the Parmesan cheese over the top.

5 Place in an oven preheated to 400°F (200°C, gas 6) and cook until set and light gold.

6 Meanwhile beat the yoghurt and garlic together in a small saucepan and heat through but do not boil.

7 Remove the egg dish from the oven, pour the yoghurt over the eggs and sprinkle with the cumin and paprika.

8 Serve immediately.


## DZEDZADZ MISSOV TZVADZEGH
*Minced meat with eggs and yoghurt*

Serve it with a bowl of fresh salad and pickles.

2 oz (50g) butter
1 onion, finely chopped
1 clove garlic, crushed
½ lb (225g) minced meat, lamb or
   beef
2 tablespoons tomato purée
½ teaspoon allspice

1 teaspoon salt
½ teaspoon black pepper
2 tablespoons chopped parsley
4 eggs
2 teaspoons paprika
½ pint (300ml) yoghurt

1 Melt half the butter in a frying pan and sauté the onion and garlic until soft.

2 Add the meat and cook well, stirring frequently.

3 Add the tomato purée, allspice, salt and pepper, and stir well.

4 Add ¼ pint (150ml) water and cook slowly for a further 15 minutes.

5 Now stir in the parsley.

6 Make four depressions in the mixture with the back of a tablespoon.

7 Break an egg into each depression.

8 Meanwhile melt the remaining butter and add the paprika.

9 Mix this with the yoghurt and then pour it over the eggs.

10 Cook slowly until the eggs are set and serve immediately.

## ANDA-DAHI KARI
### *Egg curry with yoghurt*

This is a simple but delightful dish from the Indian subcontinent. It is cheap to make and played a major part in the diet of my student days. Eat with a plain rice pilav or chapatis and chutney.

*1½ oz (40g) ghee or butter*
*1 onion, finely chopped*
*2 teaspoons turmeric*
*½ teaspoon chilli powder*
*½ teaspoon ground ginger*
*1 tablespoon* garam masala *(see p. 197)*

*1 teaspoon salt*
*½ teaspoon black pepper*
*1 teaspoon lemon juice*
*½ pint (300ml) yoghurt, stabilized*
*8 hard-boiled eggs*

1 Melt the ghee or butter in a large saucepan and sauté the onion until soft.

2 Add the turmeric, chilli powder, ginger, *garam masala*, salt and pepper.

3 Cook very gently, stirring frequently, for about 20 to 30 minutes.

4 Add the lemon juice and yoghurt, stir and heat through.

5 Shell the eggs, cut into quarters and add to the mixture.

6 Stir very gently and simmer for a further 15 minutes.

7 Serve immediately.

## SARAY YUMURTASI

*Egg and tomato, palace style*

This is an adaptation of a Turkish egg dish. It makes an excellent appetizer and looks splendid as part of a cold buffet.

4 large tomatoes
8 eggs
2 chicken breasts, cooked, boned
  and finely chopped
2 gherkins, finely sliced
24 black olives

½ pint (300ml) garlic yoghurt sauce
  (see p. 167) or Orga's yoghurt
  dressing (see p. 166)
1 teaspoon paprika
2 tablespoons chopped parsley

1 Cut the tomatoes in half and spoon out and discard the pulp.

2 Poach the eggs in water until just firm.

3 Using a slotted spoon, put one egg into each tomato half.

4 Arrange the tomatoes around a large plate leaving the centre empty.

5 Heap the chicken into the centre.

6 Chill for 1 hour.

7 Arrange the sliced gherkins and the black olives decoratively around the tomatoes.

8 Pour the yoghurt dressing over and garnish with the paprika and parsley.

9 Serve immediately.

## EGGEH MUGHRABI

*Moroccan scrambled eggs*

This is a well-loved North African egg dish normally prepared without yoghurt, but I have found yoghurt combines very well with the vegetables, enhancing them with its unique flavour.

2 oz (50g) ghee or butter
1 onion, sliced
1 clove garlic, crushed
2 tomatoes, sliced
1 green pepper, seeded and thinly
  sliced
½ teaspoon oregano

½ teaspoon chilli powder
1 teaspoon salt
¼ teaspoon black pepper
4 eggs
2 tablespoons chopped parsley
¼ pint (150ml) yoghurt

1 Melt the ghee or butter in a large frying pan, add the onion and garlic and sauté until soft.

2 Add the tomatoes, green pepper, oregano, chilli powder, salt and black pepper and cook for 10 to 15 minutes or until the vegetables are tender.

3 Place the eggs, parsley and yoghurt in a bowl and whisk.

4 Pour this mixture into the pan and cook over a low heat, stirring frequently, until set.

5 Serve immediately, with salad and bread.


## CILBIR

### *Egg on toast with spiced yoghurt*

This is a traditional Turkish recipe which makes an excellent savoury snack. The eggs are usually fried, but you can poach them if you wish.

SERVES SIX
2½ oz (65g) butter
6 eggs
6 large slices of toast
6 slices cooked tongue (optional)

½ pint (300ml) yoghurt
a level teaspoon salt
½ teaspoon black pepper
½ teaspoon cumin
1 teaspoon paprika

1 Melt 1½ oz (40g) butter in a large frying pan and break the eggs gently into the pan.

2 Cook until just firm.

3 Meanwhile arrange the rounds of toast on a large platter and place a slice of tongue on top of each.

4 Place 1 egg on top of each slice of toast.

5 Beat the yoghurt with the salt, pepper and cumin until creamy.

6 Pour a little of this mixture over each egg.

7 Melt the remaining 1 oz (25g) butter, mix with the paprika and spoon over the eggs.

8 Serve immediately.

## EGGS EN COCOTTE

Here is a yoghurt version of the French classic.

*2 rashers bacon, rind and bone*
  *removed, chopped*
*4 eggs*
*8 tablespoons yoghurt*
*salt and pepper to taste*
*2 oz (50g) grated Parmesan cheese*
*2 tablespoons chopped parsley*

**1** Divide the bacon between four ramekins or individual soufflé dishes.

**2** Bake at the top of an oven preheated to 350°F (180°C, gas 4) for 10 minutes.

**3** Break an egg into each dish.

**4** Add 2 tablespoons of yoghurt to each dish (do not let the yoghurt cover the yolks).

**5** Season with the salt and pepper.

**6** Sprinkle the cheese over the yoghurt (make sure the yoghurt is covered).

**7** Bake for 10 minutes at the top of the oven, until the eggs are lightly set.

**8** Serve in the dishes, garnished with chopped parsley.

## MACEDONIAN POACHED EGGS

This is a Balkan speciality which is also found throughout the Middle East. It makes use of spinach, which goes extremely well with yoghurt and eggs. It makes a fine hors d'oeuvre or snack meal.

*1 lb (½kg) frozen leaf spinach*
*salt*
*a little butter*
*8 eggs*

*2 cloves garlic, crushed*
*1 pint (600ml) yoghurt*
*6 oz (175g) grated Parmesan cheese*
*2 tablespoons finely chopped parsley*

**1** Thaw spinach.

**2** Place in a pan of boiling salted water and simmer for 8 to 10 minutes.

**3** Drain in a colander and, when cool enough to handle, squeeze out any excess water.

**4** Place the spinach on a wooden board and chop.

**5** Lightly butter a large shallow baking dish.

**6** Arrange the spinach in a layer over the base of the dish.

**7** With the back of a spoon make eight depressions in the spinach.

**8** Break an egg into each depression.

**9** In a small bowl mix together the garlic, yoghurt and cheese, and spoon some of the mixture over each egg.

**10** Sprinkle the parsley over the eggs.

**11** Cook under the grill until the eggs are just set and are bubbly and golden on top.

**12** Serve immediately – one egg per person if you are serving this dish as an hors d'oeuvre or two per person if it is to be served as a lunch or snack meal.

# MEAT DISHES

In the Middle East, parts of the Balkans and the north Indian subcontinent, yoghurt is not only consumed on its own or with other ingredients as part of a meal for instance, in soups and salads – but it is often cooked with meats. Lamb or mutton are still the most popular meats throughout these regions, while pork, outside the Christian lands, is completely ignored since both the Islamic and Jewish faiths forbid it. Yoghurt is also used as a side dish, with roast meats, kebabs and pilavs. Indeed, to the peasants of Turkey and Iran the greatest and tastiest meal in the world would be a bowl of rice pilav accompanied by a bowl of natural yoghurt, bread and fresh vegetables, such as cucumber, onion, tomatoes, radishes, etc. Hence the Iranian expression:

> A bowl of chelo, mast and greens to me; the keys of Paradise to thee.

### KEBABCHEH
*Meat-balls with rice in yoghurt sauce*

This Ottoman-style recipe from Bulgaria is distantly related to a dish known as *Ismir kufta*, which is made with tomatoes. It is not a true kebab as it is cooked in a saucepan. Serve with plain rice pilav and a fresh salad.

1 lb (½kg) minced meat
1 small onion, finely chopped
1 egg
4 tablespoons fresh breadcrumbs
1½ teaspoons salt
1 heaped teaspoon dried marjoram
or 1 tablespoon chopped fresh marjoram
1 pint (600ml) beef stock
2 tablespoons rice, washed
¼ pint (150ml) yoghurt
2 egg yolks

1 In a large bowl put the meat, onion, egg, breadcrumbs, salt and marjoram.

2 Knead until the mixture is smooth.

3 Divide the mixture into twenty small lumps and, with damp palms, roll them into small balls.

4 Pour the stock into a large saucepan and bring it to the boil.

5 Carefully spoon the meat-balls into the pan, cover and simmer for 15 minutes.

6 Very carefully stir in the rice and simmer for a further 20 minutes.

7 Carefully lift the meat-balls from the stock, place in a heatproof dish and keep warm.

8 In a small bowl beat the egg yolks into the yoghurt.

9 Turn the heat to very low and gradually stir the yoghurt mixture into the rice and stock.

10 Stir continuously until the sauce thickens, but do not let it boil.

11 Pour the sauce over the meat-balls and serve immediately.


## NARGISI KOFTA
### *Eggs in meat-balls*

These meat-balls look like the yellow and white flowers of the narcissus – hence their name. They are fried, then simmered in curry and served as a main dish. You can also try them fried and served hot or cold with salad as a snack lunch or for a picnic.

MEAT-BALLS
7 small eggs
1 lb (½kg) lamb or beef, minced
   twice
1 small onion, finely chopped
2 cloves garlic, crushed
½ teaspoon finely grated root ginger
1 fresh green chilli, finely chopped
1 teaspoon salt
1 teaspoon garam masala (see p. 197)
½ teaspoon turmeric

1½ tablespoons besan (chick-pea
   flour)
1 tablespoon yoghurt
oil for frying

CURRY
1 tablespoon oil
1 onion, finely chopped
5 cloves garlic, crushed
2 teaspoons finely grated fresh
   ginger

1 *teaspoon* garam masala
1 *teaspoon turmeric*
½ *teaspoon chilli powder*
2 *large ripe tomatoes*

1 *teaspoon salt*
¼ *pint (150ml) yoghurt*
2 *tablespoons chopped fresh*
   *coriander leaves (optional)*

## TO MAKE THE MEAT-BALLS

1 Put 6 eggs in a pan of cold water and bring slowly to the boil.

2 Stir the eggs gently for the first few minutes to centre the yolks.

3 Simmer for a further 5 minutes then run cold water into the pan until the eggs are cold.

4 Shell and set aside.

5 Put the meat into a saucepan with the onion, garlic, ginger, chilli, salt, *garam masala*, turmeric and ¼ pint (150ml) water.

6 Stir well, bring to the boil and then cover and simmer for 20 to 30 minutes or until the meat is well cooked.

7 Stir in the chick-pea flour and continue cooking until all the liquid has been absorbed.

8 Cool the meat mixture and then knead it until very smooth, adding a little yoghurt if necessary to moisten it and make it easier to handle.

9 Divide the mixture into six equal portions and mould each one around a hard-boiled egg.

10 Beat the remaining egg.

11 Dip the *koftas* in the beaten egg and fry in hot oil until golden brown all over.

12 Drain on kitchen paper and then cut in halves with a sharp knife. Spoon some of the curry sauce over the eggs and serve hot.

## TO MAKE THE CURRY SAUCE

1 Heat the oil in a large saucepan and fry the onion and garlic until soft and golden brown.

2 Add the ginger, *garam masala*, turmeric and chilli powder, stir for a few seconds and then add the tomatoes and salt.

3 Cover and cook to a pulp, stirring frequently.

4 Pour the yoghurt into a small bowl, beat until smooth, stir in ¼ pint (150ml) hot water and add to the curry.

5 Stir well and cook uncovered until thick.

6 If the *koftas* are prepared beforehand they can be put into the sauce to heat through and then cut in half and served with the sauce.

7 Garnish with the coriander leaves.

## KOFTA KARI
*Curried meat-balls in yoghurt*

This is one of the most popular and cheapest of all Indian curry dishes. It is a must for all festive occasions.

| | |
|---|---|
| *1 lb (½kg) minced meat* | *2 teaspoons chilli powder* |
| *2 onions* | *1 teaspoon black pepper* |
| *4 cloves garlic, peeled* | *1 teaspoon ground cumin* |
| *a handful of parsley, stalks removed* | *1 tablespoon* garam masala *(see p. 197)* |
| *1 egg* | *1 tablespoon paprika* |
| *2 teaspoons salt* | *1 teaspoon turmeric* |
| *vegetable oil for frying* | *½ oz (15g) chopped fresh ginger* |
| *2 oz (50g) ghee or butter* | *¾ pint (450ml) yoghurt* |

**1** Pass the minced meat through a mincer together with one of the onions, roughly chopped, two of the cloves of garlic and the parsley.

**2** Place this mixture in a bowl and add the egg and 1 teaspoon salt.

**3** Knead this mixture until smooth.

**4** With damp hands shape the meat into small walnut-sized balls.

**5** Heat some oil in a large frying pan and fry the balls for 2 to 3 minutes, turning and browning on all sides.

**6** Meanwhile in a large saucepan melt the ghee or butter and fry the other onion, thinly sliced, with the remaining 2 cloves garlic, finely chopped, until golden brown.

**7** Add a teaspoon of salt and the spices and cook over a low heat for about 10 minutes, stirring frequently.

**8** Add the meat-balls, cover and simmer over a low heat for 20 to 30 minutes, turning the meat-balls frequently.

**9** Remove from the heat and slowly stir in the yoghurt.

**10** Simmer gently for a further 30 to 40 minutes.

**11** Serve on a bed of rice pilav.

## BOSANSKE CUFTE
*Bosnian-style meat-balls*

This is a Yugoslav favourite of Ottoman origin. *Kufta* means minced meat in Arabic and it has passed into the Turkish language. It is distantly related to *Ismir kufta* and the Bulgarian

*Kebabcheh.* Traditional accompaniments are a rice pilav and green salad.

| | |
|---|---|
| 1 lb (½kg) minced lamb or beef | SAUCE |
| 2 oz (50g) flour | ½ pint (300ml) yoghurt |
| 1 egg | 2 eggs |
| 1 tablespoon finely chopped | 1 teaspoon caraway seeds, crushed |
|    parsley | salt and pepper to taste |
| salt and pepper to taste | ½ teaspoon ground cumin |

**1** Put the meat, flour, egg, parsley, salt and pepper into a large bowl and knead until the mixture is smooth.

**2** Keeping the palms of your hands damp, form the mixture into small balls, slightly smaller than a walnut.

**3** Grease a shallow baking dish or casserole and arrange the meat-balls in it.

**4** Cook in a preheated oven, 350°F (180°C, gas 4), for 45 minutes.

**5** Prepare the sauce by mixing together all the ingredients.

**6** Remove the baking dish from the oven and transfer the meat-balls to another shallow ovenproof dish.

**7** Pour the sauce over the meat-balls and return to the oven for a further 20 to 30 minutes until the mixture is set and golden brown.

### BORANI-YE BADEMJAN GOOSHT

*Meat-balls with aubergine in yoghurt and saffron sauce*

This was a favourite of Queen Pourandokht of Persia. It is particularly popular in the Azerbaijan region of Iran and is similar to the *kufte* (minced-meat balls) of the Balkan, Arab, Turkish and Armenian cuisines.

Serve with rice pilav.

| | |
|---|---|
| 1 large aubergine | 1 tablespoon lemon juice |
| 2 onions | ½ teaspoon ground saffron |
| 1 lb (½kg) minced beef | 1½ pints (1l) yoghurt stabilized |
| 1 teaspoon salt |    with 2 tablespoons plain flour |
| ½ teaspoon black pepper | 1 tablespoon dried mint |
| 2 oz (50g) butter | a little melted butter |
| ¼ pint (150ml) stock or water | |

1 Remove head and tail of the aubergine and peel it.

2 Quarter it lengthways and then cut crossways into ¼ in (½cm) slices.

3 Spread the slices on a large plate, sprinkle with salt and leave for ½ hour.

4 Rinse them under cold water and pat dry with kitchen paper.

5 Finely chop 1 onion and place in a large mixing bowl with the meat, salt and pepper.

6 Knead the mixture until smooth and then with damp palms shape the mixture into small meat-balls.

7 Thinly slice the remaining onion.

8 Melt 1 oz (25g) butter in a large saucepan and sauté the sliced onion until it is golden brown.

9 Add the meat-balls and sauté until browned all over, stirring frequently.

10 Add the stock and lemon juice, lower heat and simmer for about 20 minutes, stirring occasionally.

11 Meanwhile melt the remaining 1 oz (25g) butter in a large frying pan and sauté the sliced aubergine until brown on both sides. Add more butter if necessary.

12 Lightly butter a large ovenproof baking dish, arrange the meat-balls and onion in the bottom and place the aubergine slices over the top.

13 Mix the saffron into the stabilized yoghurt and pour over the meat and aubergines.

14 Place in an oven preheated to 350°F (180°C, gas 4) and bake for 20 to 30 minutes.

15 When ready to serve sauté the mint in a little melted butter for a few minutes, pour over the dish and serve immediately.

### KEEMA SEEKH KEBAB
*Minced meat on skewers*

This is a north Indian recipe for kebabs. Kebabs, of course, arrived in that subcontinent via the Middle East and Persia, but the ginger, *garam masala* and the chick-pea flour have given this recipe an authentic Indian flavour.

110

1 lb (½kg) minced lamb or beef
2 tablespoons besan (chick-pea
  flour)
1 onion, finely chopped
2 tablespoons finely chopped fresh
  coriander leaves

1 clove garlic, crushed
1 teaspoon finely grated fresh ginger
1 teaspoon salt
1 teaspoon garam masala
  (see p. 197)
2½ fl oz (75ml) yoghurt

**1** Combine the minced meat with all the other ingredients except the yoghurt.

**2** Knead until the mixture becomes very smooth.

**3** Take small handfuls of the mixture and form into sausage shapes around flat skewers.

**4** Beat the yoghurt and coat the meat with it, then place over charcoal and grill for 10 to 15 minutes, turning frequently.

**5** Serve with rice or Indian bread.


## LAMB TIKKA KEBAB

This dish, now a classic of the Indian subcontinent, was introduced by the invading Moslems from Arabia and Persia and then 'Indianized' with time. Prepare two days in advance.

2 lb (1kg) lean lamb, cut into 1 in
  (3cm) cubes

MARINADE
½ pint (300ml) yoghurt
1½ teaspoons garam masala
  (see p. 197)

½ teaspoon ground coriander
½ teaspoon turmeric
2 cloves garlic, crushed
¼ teaspoon ground nutmeg
¾ teaspoon chilli pepper
2 teaspoons ground cumin
grated rind and juice of 2 lemons

**1** Mix all the marinade ingredients together in a large bowl.

**2** Add the cubed meat, mix well, cover and leave to marinate in the refrigerator for 2 days, stirring occasionally.

**3** Thread on to skewers and grill until cooked through – about 15 to 20 minutes.

**4** Serve garnished with onion rings and lemon wedges.

**5** Eat with bread e.g. *paratha*, *lavash* or pitta.

## KABAB HALABI
*Aleppo kebab with yoghurt*

A classic of the Middle Eastern cuisine, this dish is also known as *madznov kebab* amongst the Armenians and *yogurtlu kebab* by the Turks. It originated in the region of Aleppo in northern Syria where some of the most exciting Middle Eastern dishes come from.

2 lb (1kg) lean lamb, cut into 1-in
   (3cm) cubes
2 tablespoons olive oil
juice of 1 onion
3 pitta breads
2 oz (50g) ghee or butter, melted

3 large tomatoes
½ teaspoon salt
¾ pint (450ml) yoghurt
6 spring onions, finely chopped
1 tablespoon parsley, finely chopped

**1** Put the meat into a large bowl, add the oil and onion juice, mix well and leave to marinate for 2 hours at room temperature.

**2** Just before you cook the kebabs warm the pittas over the fire and then cut them into ½ in (1cm) wide strips and place on a large serving platter.

**3** Pour the melted butter over the bread, mix well, arrange the pieces neatly and set aside to keep warm.

**4** Thread the pieces of meat on skewers and grill for about 15 minutes, turning frequently.

**5** Meanwhile peel and chop the tomatoes.

**6** Put the chopped tomatoes into a small frying pan and cook gently for about 3 minutes.

**7** Season with the salt.

**8** When the kebabs are cooked first pour the tomatoes over the bread and then slide the meat off the skewers on to the tomatoes.

**9** Pour the yoghurt over the meat.

**10** Sprinkle the chopped onion and parsley over the top and serve immediately.

## KHOZI TAP-TAP
*Minced pork and burghul kebab*

This dish comes from Sis, the capital of Cilician Armenia.

*8 oz (250g) fine* burghul
*1 lb (½kg) lean pork, minced*
*1 onion, very finely chopped*
*2 teaspoons cumin*
*1 teaspoon oregano*

*salt and pepper to taste*
*2 oz (50g) sesame seeds*
*½ pint (300ml) yoghurt*
*½ teaspoon chilli powder*
*1 clove garlic, finely chopped*

1 Soak the *burghul* in cold water for 10 minutes.

2 Drain in a fine sieve.

3 In a large bowl place the *burghul*, meat, onion, cumin, oregano, salt and pepper.

4 Knead the mixture for about 10 minutes, dampening your hands with cold water occasionally.

5 Divide the mixture into four portions and with your hands mould each one into a circle about 6 ins (15cm) in diameter and ½ in (1cm) thick.

6 Before cooking sprinkle some sesame seeds on both sides of the *tap-tap*.

7 Cook over charcoal, turning frequently to prevent burning. This should take about 10 minutes.

8 When cooked, serve on a plate topped with a mixture of fresh yoghurt, chilli powder and garlic.

9 Serve with a plate of fresh salad or pickles.

### Amram

Another favourite from Sis makes use of minced leg of lamb or beef. Follow the recipe above, but omit oregano, and sesame seed and substitute lamb for pork.

## VEAL IN YOGHURT KEBAB

This light and extremely tasty veal kebab is marinated in yoghurt.

*⅓ pint (200ml) yoghurt*
*1 clove garlic, crushed*
*1 large onion, finely chopped*
*salt and pepper to taste*
*1 lb (½kg) shoulder of veal, cut into*
*   1 in (3cm) cubes*

*2 onions, quartered*
*3 tomatoes, halved*
*1 green pepper, white pith and seeds*
*   removed, cut into 8 pieces*
*1 teaspoon paprika*

**1** Mix the yoghurt, garlic, chopped onion, salt and pepper together in a large bowl.

**2** Add the meat, mix well, cover and leave to marinate for 4 to 6 hours.

**3** Thread the meat on to skewers alternating the meat with the onion quarters, halved tomatoes and pepper pieces.

**4** Cook over charcoal or under the grill for 15 to 20 minutes. If the meat looks as though it is drying, brush with a little olive oil.

**5** Slide the kebabs on to a plate and sprinkle with the paprika.

**6** Heat up the remaining marinade, but do not boil, and serve as an accompanying sauce.

## YOGHURT MOUSSAKA

Here is a variation of the traditional moussaka found on any self-respecting Greek restaurant menu.

*2 oz (50g) butter*
*1 clove garlic, crushed*
*1 onion, finely chopped*
*2 large aubergines*
*1 lb (½kg) tomatoes, fresh or*
*   canned, roughly chopped; include*
*   the juice if using canned ones*
*1 teaspoon dried oregano or 1*
*   tablespoon fresh oregano*

*¾ lb (350g) minced lamb or beef*
*½ teaspoon dried rosemary or ½*
*   tablespoon fresh rosemary*
*1 teaspoon salt*
*½ teaspoon black pepper*
*½ pint (300ml) yoghurt*
*1 egg yolk*
*1 tablespoon Parmesan cheese,*
*   grated*

1 Melt the butter in a large ovenproof casserole.

2 Add the garlic and onion and sauté until soft and transparent.

3 Cut the heads and tails off the aubergines and cut lengthways into ¼ in (½cm) slices.

4 Add the aubergine slices to the casserole and cook for about 10 minutes, stirring frequently. Add a little more butter if necessary.

5 Add the tomatoes, meat, oregano, rosemary, salt and pepper.

6 Cover and simmer for 30 to 45 minutes or until the meat is cooked.

7 Place the yoghurt and egg yolk in a small pan and beat vigorously.

8 Cook over a low heat for about 10 minutes, stirring continuously.

9 Pour this yoghurt sauce over the meat and vegetables and sprinkle the cheese over the top.

10 Place in an oven preheated to 350°F (180°C, gas 4) and cook for about 30 minutes.

11 Serve immediately.

## CZANGO GOULASH
### *Gypsy-style goulash*

Needless to say this is a Hungarian speciality – with a difference in that it does not contain all the ingredients traditionally associated with goulash: onions, paprika, potatoes and pasta. *Czango* has sauerkraut, rice and caraway seeds, which give it its distinctive flavour. I have substituted yoghurt for the traditional soured cream.

*2 oz (50g) lard or butter*
*1 onion, thinly sliced*
*1 clove garlic, crushed*
*1 tablespoon paprika*
*1 tablespoon caraway seeds*
*2 lb (1kg) sirloin steak, cut into 2 in (5cm) pieces*
*2 teaspoons salt*

*1 lb (½kg) sauerkraut (commercial makes will do fine)*
*2 green peppers, seeded and sliced*
*3 oz (75g) rice, washed thoroughly*
*1 pint (600ml) yoghurt, stabilized with 1 egg or 1 tablespoon plain flour*

1 Melt the lard or butter in a large saucepan and fry the onion and garlic until golden brown.

2 Add the paprika, caraway seeds, ½ pint (300ml) water, and the

meat and salt, stir, cover and allow to simmer gently for about 1½ hours.

3 Wash the sauerkraut under cold running water and add to the pan together with the sliced green peppers.

4 Add sufficient water to cover and continue cooking until the meat is tender.

5 Add the rice, stir and cook for a further 10 to 12 minutes.

6 Just before serving fold in the yoghurt and heat through but do not boil.

7 Serve immediately.

## MARJORAM TOKÁNY

A really delicious stew from Budapest which gains its distinctive flavour from the addition of marjoram.

*2 lb (1kg) beef steak, fillet, sirloin or rump*
*2 oz (50g) lard*
*2 onions, finely chopped*
*2 tablespoons chopped fresh marjoram or 1 tablespoon dried marjoram*
*1 teaspoon salt*
*½ teaspoon black pepper*
*½ pint (300ml) dry white wine*
*8 oz (250g) smoked bacon rashers, rind and bones removed*
*1 clove garlic, crushed*
*1 pint (600ml) yoghurt stabilized with 1 egg or 1 tablespoon plain flour*
*2 tablespoons chopped fresh parsley for garnish*

1 Remove any excess fat and then cut the meat into long slices ½ in (1cm) thick.

2 Melt the lard in a large saucepan, add the onions and fry until golden brown.

3 Add the slices of meat, marjoram, salt and pepper, and cook for a few minutes, stirring very frequently.

4 Stir in the wine and simmer gently for about 15 minutes.

5 Meanwhile cut the bacon into strips and fry in a small frying pan for a few minutes and then add to the stew, together with the garlic.

6 Add a few tablespoons of the hot sauce to the yoghurt and then stir the yoghurt slowly into the stew.

7 Continue to simmer gently for 20 to 30 minutes or until the meat is tender.

**8** Serve garnished with the parsley and accompanied by boiled potatoes or a rice pilav.

### RAMA'S BATH

I find fascinating not only the name of this dish but also the fact that it is the only recipe incorporating yoghurt that I have been able to trace from Thailand. I suspect that it is a dish of Indian origin which has been taken over and adapted by the Thais.

COCONUT MILK
*½ lb (250g) desiccated coconut*

PASTE MIXTURE
*3 cloves garlic*
*3 spring onions*
*1 teaspoon roughly chopped root ginger*
*3 fresh chilli peppers*
*1 tablespoon lime or lemon juice*
*salt to taste*

*1 lb (½kg) beef steak*
*1 tablespoon brown sugar*
*1 tablespoon roasted nuts, finely chopped (e.g. peanuts, almonds or walnuts)*
*1 tablespoon soy sauce*
*2 tablespoons flour*
*1 teaspoon salt*
*1 lb (½kg) fresh or frozen spinach*
*¼–½ pint (150–300ml) yoghurt, depending on taste*

TO MAKE THE COCONUT MILK (a simplified recipe)

**1** Soak the coconut in ½ pint (300ml) water for about 10 minutes.

**2** Strain off the liquid and retain it.

**3** Repeat steps 1 and 2 twice more.

**4** When you have almost 1½ pints (1l) of the liquid, boil it in a saucepan for about 10 minutes until it is reduced slightly.

TO MAKE THE PASTE MIXTURE

**1** Put all the ingredients in the goblet of the liquidizer and blend until smooth.

**1** Cut the meat into ½ in (1 cm) slices.

**2** Put the coconut milk, sugar, nuts and soy sauce into a large saucepan.

**3** Add the meat, bring to the boil then lower the heat and simmer.

**4** Mix the flour to a smooth paste with a little water and stir into the saucepan.

**5** Then add the paste mixture to the pan, stir thoroughly, season with salt, cover and simmer until the meat is tender and the sauce has thickened.

**6** If using fresh spinach wash it very thoroughly until all the sand and gravel has been removed. If using frozen spinach then thaw it out.

**7** Half fill a large pan with boiling salted water, add the spinach and cook for about 10 minutes.

**8** Drain the spinach, squeeze out excess moisture and arrange on a large serving plate.

**9** Spoon the meat and sauce over the spinach and then pour the yoghurt over the top.

**10** Serve immediately with a plain rice pilav.

### MADZNOV HORTIMISS
*Beef with yoghurt*

This Armenian dish is usually made with soured cream, but I think that yoghurt adds an extra dimension to the flavour. Traditionally, pickled grapes and apples are served as a garnish or side dish.

*2 lb (1kg) beef, fillet or sirloin*
*1 teaspoon salt*
*½ teaspoon black pepper*
*2 oz (50g) ghee or unsalted butter*
*1 teaspoon ground cloves*
*1 pint (600ml) yoghurt stabilized*

*with 1 egg or 1 tablespoon plain flour*
*1 tablespoon* sumak *powder (see p. 198)*
*pickled apples and pickled grapes for garnish*

**1** Trim the beef of all fat and gristle.

**2** Cut the beef into ½ in (1cm) slices and pound thin with a mallet.

**3** Sprinkle the meat with the salt and pepper.

**4** Melt the ghee in a large pan and sauté the meat slices quickly over a moderate heat for 1 to 2 minutes only, turning once.

**5** Sprinkle the meat with the cloves, add the yoghurt and toss gently.

**6** Cover the pan and simmer for about 10 to 15 minutes.

**7** Transfer the meat to a large shallow dish, pour the sauce over the top, sprinkle with the *sumak* and serve immediately.

**8** Garnish with the pickled apples and grapes and serve with a pila**v**.

## DRY BEEF CURRY

A curry to eat with chapatis rather than rice. It may be made with lamb instead of beef, but should then be cooked for 45 minutes to 1 hour.

*4 tablespoons vegetable oil*
*2 green chillies, finely chopped*
*2 onions, finely chopped*
*2 lb (1kg) beef steak, cut into ½ in*
*   (1cm) cubes*
*½ teaspoon salt*
*2 tomatoes, blanched, peeled and*
*   chopped*

*1 teaspoon turmeric*
*1 teaspoon cumin*
*2 teaspoons ground coriander*
*1½ teaspoons* garam masala
*   (see p. 197)*
*½ pint (300ml) stabilized yoghurt*
*1 tablespoon chopped fresh coriander*
*   leaves*

**1** Heat the oil in a saucepan, add the chillies and fry for 1 minute.

**2** Add the onions and fry until soft, but not brown.

**3** Add the beef cubes and salt and fry, stirring frequently, until the meat is browned on all sides.

**4** Reduce the heat and add the tomatoes.

**5** Continue cooking for 10 minutes or until most of the tomato liquid has evaporated.

**6** In a small bowl combine the turmeric, cumin, ground coriander, and 1 teaspoon of the *garam masala*.

**7** Add the yoghurt and continue beating until yoghurt and spices are well blended.

**8** Add this to the meat mixture in the saucepan and stir well.

**9** Half cover the pan, reduce heat to low and simmer the curry for 1½ hours.

**10** Remove the lid from the pan and continue cooking for a further 30 minutes or until the liquid has evaporated leaving the meat in a thick sauce.

**11** If it becomes too dry cover the pan and continue cooking.

**12** Spoon the curry into a serving dish and sprinkle the top with the remaining *garam masala* and coriander leaves.

## ROGHAN JOSH
*Lamb in yoghurt and spices*

Kashmiri dishes make great use of yoghurt. There are several recipes for *roghan josh*, but this is my favourite – and an added bonus is that it is a little simpler to prepare than some of the others. Chapatis, *parathas* or even pitta bread will make an excellent accompaniment.

½ pint (300ml) yoghurt
1 oz (25g) ghee or butter, melted
2 teaspoons salt
1 teaspoon ground ginger
2 lb (1kg) lean lamb, cut into 1 in (3cm) pieces

1½ teaspoons chilli powder
1 teaspoon ground cumin
2 teaspoons garam masala (see p. 197)
2 tablespoons chopped fresh coriander leaves (optional)

**1** Mix the yoghurt, ghee, salt and ginger together in a large saucepan.

**2** Add the meat cubes, turn until they are well coated and then cover and simmer for a few minutes, stirring occasionally.

**3** After about 5 minutes you will notice that the juices are evaporating. Stir in about ¼ pint (150ml) water, together with the chilli powder and cumin.

**4** Simmer for about 10 to 15 minutes, stirring frequently, until the water has evaporated.

**5** Add a little more water and simmer for a further 10 to 15 minutes.

**6** Continue cooking the meat in this way until it is tender.

**7** Add the *garam masala* and coriander leaves, stir and simmer for another 10 to 15 minutes, stirring very frequently.

**8** Pile on to a large plate and serve immediately.

## KORMA
*Spiced lamb in yoghurt*

This Indian dish has a delicate flavour, yet is full of fascinating spices. Serve with a plain rice pilav.

2 onions
1 tablespoon chopped fresh root ginger
1 clove garlic

1 oz (25g) cashew nuts
4 dried chillies, seeds removed and discarded
2 teaspoons ground coriander

½ teaspoon ground cumin
¼ teaspoon ground cardamon
¼ teaspoon ground cloves
2 oz (50g) butter
2 teaspoons salt
½ teaspoon ground saffron

2 lb (1kg) leg of lamb, cut into 1 in
   (3cm) pieces
¼ pint (150ml) stabilized yoghurt
2 tablespoons chopped coriander
   leaves or parsley

**1** Peel the onions, slice one and chop the other finely.

**2** Put the chopped onion into a liquidizer with the ginger, garlic, cashew nuts, chillies, coriander, cumin, cardamon, cloves and ¼ pint (150ml) water and blend until smooth.

**3** Melt the butter in a large saucepan or casserole, add the sliced onion and cook until golden brown.

**4** Add the blended spices, ¼ pint (150ml) water and the salt and continue cooking until much of the liquid has evaporated.

**5** Add the meat and mix well until the meat cubes are well coated with the spices.

**6** Mix the saffron with 2 to 3 tablespoons of boiling water and leave for a few minutes.

**7** Stir the saffron into the meat mixture.

**8** Add the yoghurt and mix thoroughly.

**9** Reduce the heat, cover and simmer for about 1 hour until the meat is very tender. Stir occasionally to prevent sticking.

**10** Sprinkle with the coriander or parsley and cook for a further 5 minutes.

**11** Spoon into a dish and serve immediately.

## JAGNJECA KAPAMA S JAJIMA
### Lamb and egg casserole

This is a dish from Yugoslavia; it owes its origin to the Turkish Ottoman domination of that country. It is a rich, tasty stew and looks attractive on a dinner table with its golden crust.
   Serve with boiled potatoes or pitta bread.

1½ lb (¾kg) boned leg of lamb, cut
   into 1 in (3cm) pieces
salt and pepper to taste

2 tablespoons flour
4 tablespoons olive oil
1 large onion, finely chopped

1 large leek, trimmed, washed
   carefully and chopped – including
   some of the green tops

½ pint (300ml) water or stock
2–3 eggs
½ pint (300ml) yoghurt

**1** Sprinkle some salt and pepper over the meat cubes and coat them with the flour.

**2** Heat the oil in a large casserole and fry the lamb cubes, turning frequently, until they are browned all over.

**3** With a slotted spoon remove the meat cubes and transfer to a plate.

**4** Add the onion and leek to the pan and fry, stirring occasionally, for about 10 minutes.

**5** Return the meat to the pan and stir in the water or stock.

**6** Bring to the boil, cover and cook in an oven preheated to 325°F (160°C, gas 3) for about 1½ hours or until the meat is tender.

**7** Beat the eggs thoroughly into the yoghurt and then pour it into the casserole.

**8** Return to the oven and cook for a further 30 minutes or until it is golden and set firm.


## BORANI – YE GOOSHT
### *Lentil stew with yoghurt*

This is a typical Middle Eastern stew with the added Iranian touches of saffron and oregano. It is equally delicious hot or cold, so you can serve it as an hors d'oeuvre or as a main dish.

1 large aubergine
1 oz (25g) butter
1 onion, finely chopped
1 lb (½kg) shoulder of lamb, cut into
   small pieces
1 pint (600ml) stock
1 teaspoon salt

½ teaspoon black pepper
½ teaspoon saffron diluted in 1
   tablespoon hot water
1 teaspoon oregano
3 oz (75g) whole brown lentils, rinsed
1 pint (600ml) yoghurt
1 clove garlic, finely chopped

**1** Peel the aubergine, cut in half lengthways and then cut crossways into ¼ in (½cm) slices.

**2** Arrange the slices over a large plate, sprinkle with salt and set aside for 30 minutes.

**3** Then drain, rinse and dry with kitchen paper.

**4** Melt the butter in a large saucepan and sauté the onion until golden brown.

**5** Add the meat and cook for a few minutes, turning frequently.

**6** Add the stock, salt, pepper, saffron and oregano and bring to the boil.

**7** Cover and simmer for 1 hour.

**8** Add the lentils to the pan, cover and simmer for a further 30 minutes or until all the ingredients are tender. Add more water if necessary.

**9** Add the aubergine slices, cover again and simmer for a further 20 to 30 minutes.

**10** At this stage you can serve the stew with the yoghurt stirred through it.

**11** However, it is usual to cool the stew slightly and then liquidize it or pound it to a paste in a large mortar and pestle.

**12** The yoghurt is then stirred into the pulp and the garlic is sprinkled over the top.

**13** Serve cold with bread (e.g. pitta) or hot with a rice pilav.

### TAH CHIN
*Baked rice and lamb casserole*

This dish, the name of which means literally 'arranged on the bottom of the pan', is one of the great classics of the Iranian cuisine. It makes a wholesome meal and is very attractive in appearance.

**SERVES SIX**

¾ pint (450ml) yoghurt
1 large onion, sliced
1 teaspoon ground saffron
1 tablespoon lemon juice
1 teaspoon salt
½ teaspoon black pepper

2–3 lb (1–1½kg) leg of lamb, boned
2 tablespoons salt
1 lb (500g) basmati rice, washed
   thoroughly
2 egg yolks
3 oz (75g) butter, melted

**1** In a large bowl mix together the yoghurt, onion, half the saffron, lemon juice, salt and pepper.

**2** Add the meat, turn to ensure it is well coated and then leave to marinate overnight.

**3** Remove the meat from the marinade, place in a roasting tin and bake in an oven preheated to 350°F (180°C, gas 4) for about 2 hours, or until tender. Reserve the marinade.

**4** Allow the meat to cool and then cut into thick slices.

**5** Threequarters fill a large saucepan with water and bring to the boil.

**6** Add the 2 tablespoons of salt and pour in the rice slowly so that the water does not go off the boil. Stir once.

**7** Boil for 6 minutes, drain into a colander, rinse with cold water and drain again.

**8** Put half of the rice into a bowl and mix in the marinade and the egg yolks.

**9** Put half the melted butter in the bottom of a saucepan and then spread the rice mixture over the bottom of the pan.

**10** Arrange the slices of meat over the rice and then cover with the remaining rice.

**11** Place a tea-towel over the top of the pan and then fit on the lid.

**12** Steam over a very low heat for about 45 minutes.

**13** Dissolve the remaining saffron in 1 tablespoon of hot water.

**14** Remove 4 tablespoons of the cooked rice from the top of the pan, place in a small bowl, add the saffron mixture and stir until the rice is golden.

**15** Empty out the rice and meat on to a large serving plate, garnish with the saffron rice and pour the remaining melted butter over the top.

**16** There will be a thick, crisp crust of rice (*tah-dig*) at the bottom of the pan. To remove it in one piece stand the pan in 2 in (5cm) cold water for 2 to 3 minutes and then lift out with a spatula. Cut into pieces and arrange around the edge of the serving plate.

### BANJA A JAGNJETINOM
*Lamb and okra casserole with yoghurt*

Okra – or ladies' fingers – is a popular Indo-Iranian vegetable that has spread throughout the Middle East. This dish is popular, in one form or another, throughout the Balkans and

Near and Middle East. It uses yoghurt as an essential accompaniment.

*1 lb (½kg) fresh okra*
*juice of 1 lemon*
*4 tablespoons olive or vegetable oil*
*1 onion, finely chopped*
*1½ lb (¾kg) lamb cut into 1-in (3cm) pieces*
*1 heaped tablespoon flour*
*½ teaspoon black pepper*

*½ teaspoon cayenne pepper*
*1 teaspoon salt*
*2 tablespoons finely chopped parsley*
*2–3 large tomatoes, blanched, peeled and sliced*
*1 pint (600ml) garlic yoghurt sauce (see p. 167)*

**1** Wash okra and remove stem by cutting the thin cone-shaped skin off the top – take care not to cut through the shell of the vegetable because then the juice would run out.

**2** Put the okra into a bowl and sprinkle with a little salt and a little of the lemon juice.

**3** Shake the bowl to mix well.

**4** Heat the oil in a large casserole, add the onion and the meat cubes and fry, turning frequently, until golden brown.

**5** Stir in the flour, black and cayenne peppers, salt, parsley and ½ pint (300ml) water.

**6** Bring to the boil, lower heat and simmer, covered, for about 1 hour or until the meat is just tender.

**7** Add the okra, the rest of the lemon juice and the tomatoes, stir gently and then simmer, uncovered, for a further ½ hour or until the okra is tender. Take care not to overcook or the okra will lose its shape.

**8** Serve immediately, with the garlic yoghurt sauce in a separate bowl.

### BADAMI GOSHT
#### *Lamb with saffron and almonds*

This recipe from northern India was undoubtedly Iranian in origin. It is a most attractive and beautifully coloured dish, which is very spicy but by no means hot.

A saffron rice pilav is an excellent accompaniment, as is *jajig* – the yoghurt and cucumber salad on p. 65.

½ teaspoon saffron strands soaked
   in 2 tablespoons hot water
½ pint (300ml) yoghurt stabilized
   with 1 egg or 1 tablespoon plain
   flour
1½ teaspoons salt
2 lb (1kg) boned lamb, excess fat
   removed and the meat cut into 1
   in (3cm) cubes
2 oz (50g) ghee or butter

1 small stick cinnamon
3 whole cloves
1 onion, finely chopped
2 cloves garlic, finely chopped
1 teaspoon grated fresh ginger
1 teaspoon ground cumin
3 cardamon pods (optional)
1½ tablespoons ground almonds
1 tablespoon chopped fresh mint

**1** Squeeze the saffron strands in their water to release as much of the colour and fragrance as possible.

**2** Put the yoghurt into a large bowl and stir in the saffron water and salt.

**3** Add the meat cubes, turn until coated with the mixture and then set aside.

**4** In a large saucepan or casserole melt the ghee, add the cinnamon stick and cloves and fry for a few minutes.

**5** Add the onion, garlic and ginger, and fry gently for a few minutes until the onions are golden brown.

**6** Now add the cumin and fry for 2 more minutes.

**7** Drain the pieces of meat from the marinade, but reserve the marinade; add the meat to the pan and toss in the spices until well coated.

**8** Stir in the yoghurt marinade, almonds, cardamon pods and ½ pint (300ml) water, lower the heat and simmer for about 1 hour or until the lamb is tender and the sauce is thick. Stir frequently to prevent the meat from sticking to the pan.

**9** Stir in the mint and serve immediately on a bed of rice pilav.

## RAAN

### *Roast leg of lamb in yoghurt*

This is a delightful Kashmiri dish. The meat is full of flavour and it is best served with a plain rice pilav and a garnish of sliced cucumber and tomatoes.

1 leg of lamb, approximately 3–4 lb
  (1½–2kg), boned and with excess
  fat removed
1 teaspoon grated fresh ginger
2 cloves garlic, finely chopped
2 teaspoons salt
½ teaspoon ground cumin
½ teaspoon turmeric
½ teaspoon cinnamon
½ teaspoon ground cardamon

½ teaspoon chilli powder
1 tablespoon lemon juice
1 tablespoon olive oil
¼ pint (150ml) yoghurt
1 tablespoon blanched almonds
1 tablespoon pistachio or cashew
  nuts
¼ teaspoon ground saffron
2 teaspoons honey

1 Make several deep incisions all over the leg of lamb.

2 Mix together in a bowl the ginger, garlic, salt, cumin, turmeric, cinnamon, cardamon, chilli powder, lemon juice and olive oil.

3 Rub this mixture over the lamb, especially into the slits.

4 Put the yoghurt, almonds, nuts, saffron and honey into a liquidizer and blend.

5 Place the lamb in a deep dish and pour the yoghurt mixture over it.

6 Cover and leave for 6 to 8 hours or overnight in the refrigerator. Spread marinade over meat before and during marination.

7 Turn the lamb once or twice while it is marinating.

8 Preheat oven to 350°F (180°C, gas 4).

9 Place the lamb and any remaining marinade in a roasting dish and cook for approximately 2 hours or until cooked through.

10 Serve with a plain pilav.


## KHORAK-E-KASHK-BADEMJAN
### Aubergine casserole

This casserole was traditionally made with liquid whey, *kashk*, but nowadays yoghurt is almost always used instead. Yellow split peas, turmeric and walnuts give it an exotic flavour. It is a popular Iranian dish from the region of Kerman. It is always accompanied by a bowl of rice pilav.

3 oz (75g) ghee or butter
2 onions, thinly sliced
1½ lb (¾kg) lean lamb cut into
  pieces

1 pint (600ml) stock
1 teaspoon salt
1½ tablespoons tomato purée mixed
  with ¼ pint (150ml) warm water

½ teaspoon black pepper
2 oz (50g) split peas, soaked
   overnight in cold water
1 aubergine

½ pint (300ml) yoghurt
½ teaspoon turmeric
1 oz (25g) chopped walnuts

1 Melt 1 oz (25g) ghee or butter in a large saucepan.

2 Add the onions and fry until soft and golden brown.

3 Add the pieces of meat and fry, stirring frequently, until brown all over.

4 Stir in the stock, salt, pepper and diluted tomato purée.

5 Bring to the boil, cover and simmer for about 45 minutes.

6 Then add the split peas and cook for a further 15 to 20 minutes or until peas are just tender.

7 Meanwhile cut the top off the aubergine and peel it.

8 Cut it in half lengthwise and slice crosswise into ¼ in (½cm) pieces.

9 Lay them on a large plate, sprinkle with salt and leave for 30 minutes.

10 Rinse the pieces under cold water and dry on kitchen paper.

11 Melt the remaining 2 oz (50g) butter in a large frying pan and sauté the aubergine slices until they are brown on both sides.

12 Drain on kitchen paper to remove excess fat.

13 Pour the meat and pea mixture into a baking dish and arrange the aubergine slices over the top.

14 Bake in a preheated oven (350°F, 180°C, gas 4) for about 40 minutes.

15 Mix the yoghurt and turmeric together in a small bowl. Stir in 2 or 3 tablespoons of the hot sauce and then pour over the meat and aubergines.

16 Sprinkle with the walnuts and serve immediately.

## YOGURTLU PAÇA

### Sheep's feet with yoghurt

This very old recipe from the Middle East is popular among Armenians and Turks. It is a rich, earthy, peasant dish, full of flavour.

6 sheep's feet
1½ tablespoons lemon rind
2 cloves garlic, roughly chopped
1 tablespoon olive oil
2 teaspoons salt
2 oz (50g) butter
8 pieces bread – either thin sliced
  bread with crusts removed or pitta
  breads each cut into quarters
1 pint (600ml) yoghurt

2 cloves garlic, crushed
a knob of butter
1 teaspoon paprika

GARNISH
1 small cucumber, thinly sliced
1 teaspoon lemon juice
1 teaspoon roughly chopped fresh
  mint leaves

**1** Scrub the feet thoroughly and wash several times under running water.

**2** Bring a large pan, half filled with water, to the boil, carefully drop the feet in and blanch for about 10 minutes. Then drain.

**3** Return the feet to the pan, add 5 pints (3l) water, or more if this is not enough to cover. Add the lemon rind, chopped garlic, olive oil and salt.

**4** Bring to the boil and spoon off the scum.

**5** Reduce the heat to the barest minimum and simmer for about 4 hours. Add more water if necessary.

**6** Remove the feet, but retain the stock, and when they are cool enough to handle strip all the meat from the bones.

**7** Melt the 2 oz (50g) butter in a frying pan and fry the bread until golden brown and crisp.

**8** Arrange these bread slices over the bottom of a large shallow ovenproof dish.

**9** Spread the meat over the bread and keep in a warm oven.

**10** Spoon several tablespoons of the hot stock into the yoghurt and crushed garlic and stir well; then pour the yoghurt into the stock and heat through but do not boil.

**11** Pour this sauce over the meat and bread.

**12** Melt the knob of butter in a small pan, add the paprika and stir.

**13** Dribble this butter-paprika sauce over the dish.

**14** Serve immediately with a side salad made up of sliced cucumber tossed in the lemon juice and mint leaves.

## KOURZA
*Dumplings stuffed with meat*

This is a Caucasian recipe from Azerbaijan related to *manti* – a ravioli-type dumpling – which is characteristic of the Mongolian cuisine. The dumplings were usually made in advance and cooked whenever the nomads had time to stop. It is a convenient and versatile dish as it can be made into a soup – as with *mantabour* (see p. 41) – or a main dish as here.

**DOUGH**
8 oz (250g) plain flour
2 eggs
pinch of salt

**FILLING**
1 oz (25g) butter

½ lb (250g) minced lamb or beef
1 onion, finely chopped
1 teaspoon salt
½ teaspoon black pepper
½ teaspoon cinnamon
1 pint (600ml) yoghurt
1 clove garlic, optional

1  First prepare the dough. Place the flour in a large mixing bowl and make a hollow in the middle.

2  Add the eggs, 4 tablespoons of water and the salt.

3  Mix the ingredients together until a dough is formed. Add a little more water if necessary.

4  Form the dough into a ball.

5  Sprinkle some flour on to a working surface and then knead the dough for 10 to 15 minutes, adding a little more flour if the dough becomes sticky.

6  Cover with a tea-towel and leave to rest for about 30 minutes.

7  Meanwhile melt the butter in a saucepan, add the meat and onion and sauté until the meat turns dark brown, stirring frequently.

8  Season with the salt and pepper and remove from the heat.

9  For convenience, divide the dough into two or three balls.

10  Roll out one of the balls on a floured surface until paper thin.

11  Cut out as many 3 in (8cm) circles as possible.

12  Repeat with the remaining balls of dough.

13  Place about 1 teaspoon of the meat mixture in the lower half of each circle of dough.

14  Dip a finger in cold water and run it around the edge of the circle.

15  Fold the top half over the lower half to make a half moon.

16  Seal the edges with the prongs of a fork.

17  Boil some water, with 1 teaspoon of salt, in a large saucepan.

**18** Drop in some of the dumplings, about six or eight at a time, and simmer for about 10 minutes or until the dumplings rise to the surface.
**19** Transfer the cooked dumplings to kitchen paper to drain and then keep them warm.
**20** Repeat until all the dumplings are cooked.
**21** Place all the dumplings in a large serving dish and sprinkle with the cinnamon.
**22** Serve accompanied by a bowl of yoghurt flavoured with the garlic if desired.

## KUTAB
### *Lamb pastries*

This popular recipe from the Caucasus is actually of Mongolian origin. The pastries are fried in butter and served with *sumak* and yoghurt. A fresh mixed salad is all you need to accompany this dish.

DOUGH
*8 oz (250g) plain flour*
*2 eggs*
*pinch of salt*

FILLING
*½ lb (250g) minced lamb*
*1 small onion, finely chopped*
*2 tablespoons fresh pomegranate*

*juice or 1 teaspoon commercial concentrated pomegranate juice*
*pinch of cinnamon*
*salt and pepper to taste*
*¼–½ pint (150–300ml) vegetable oil*
*2 tablespoons* sumak *(see p. 198)*
*¾ pint (450ml) yoghurt*

**1** First prepare the dough. Place the flour in a large mixing bowl and make a hollow in the middle.
**2** Add the eggs, 4 tablespoons of water and the salt.
**3** Mix the ingredients together until a dough is formed. Add a little more water if necessary.
**4** Form the dough into a ball.
**5** Sprinkle some flour on a flat working surface and knead the dough for 10 to 15 minutes, adding a little more flour if it becomes sticky.
**6** Cover with a tea-towel and leave to rest for 30 minutes.
**7** Meanwhile put all the ingredients for the filling into a large bowl and knead until well blended and smooth.

8 For convenience divide the dough into two balls.

9 Roll out one of the balls on a floured surface until paper thin.

10 Cut into circles 3 in (8cm) in diameter.

11 Repeat with the remaining ball of dough.

12 Place about 1 teaspoon of the meat mixture in the lower half of each circle of dough.

13 Dip a finger in cold water and run it around the edge of the circle.

14 Fold the top half over the lower half to make a half moon.

15 Seal the edges with the prongs of a fork.

16 In a large frying pan or saucepan heat the vegetable oil.

17 Add a few of the pastries and fry gently until golden brown. Do not fry too quickly or the meat inside will not be cooked.

18 Cook the remaining pastries in the same way, keeping those already cooked warm under the grill or in the oven. You may find it necessary to add more oil from time to time.

19 Serve all the pastries on a large plate with the *sumak* sprinkled over the top.

20 Either serve the yoghurt in a separate bowl or spooned over the pastries.

### Variation

In Azerbaijan steamed and puréed pumpkin is often used as a filling.

*1 small pumpkin, 2–3 lb (1–1½kg)*  *2 tablespoons fresh pomegranate*
*1 onion, finely chopped*  *juice or 1 teaspoon concentrated*
*½ teaspoon cinnamon*  *juice*
*salt and pepper to taste*

1 Remove the skin and seeds from the pumpkin as you would from a melon.

2 Cut the flesh into small pieces.

3 Place in a large saucepan with 1½ teaspoons of salt and sufficient water to cover.

4 Bring to the boil and simmer until very soft.

5 Drain and mash the pumpkin to a purée.

6 Fry the onion in a little vegetable oil until soft.

7 Place the pumpkin purée in a large bowl with the fried onion, pomegranate juice, cinnamon and salt and pepper to taste.

8 Mix together and then proceed to make the pastries as described above.

# POULTRY

## DAPAKHAV MADZNOV
### *Fried chicken with a prune and yoghurt sauce*

This is a classic Caucasian recipe. It is known among Georgians as *tabaka* and among Armenians as *dabakadz hav*. I have adapted it very slightly to incorporate yoghurt and to my delight have found that it works beautifully.

4 poussins (1–1½ lb, 500–700g), washed and dried
2 tablespoons salt
¼ pint (150ml) yoghurt
3 oz (75g) ghee or butter
3 tomatoes, thinly sliced
1 small aubergine, cut in half lengthways and then cut crossways into ¼ in (½cm) slices
1 clove garlic, crushed
½ teaspoon ground cinnamon
¼–½ pint (150–300ml) tkemali sauce (see p. 172)

1 Place a poussin on a chopping board, back upwards.

2 With a sharp pointed knife start at the neck and cut along one side of the backbone.

3 Turn the poussin around and cut along the other side of the backbone thus freeing it.

4 Break it away from the spoon-shaped bone connecting the breasts and remove both the bones and the white cartilage.

5 Loosen the skin around the leg and thigh and push it back exposing the thigh joint. Cut it half across and pull the skin back. Repeat with the other leg.

6 Make a small slit in each breast below the ribs.

7 Turn the poussin flesh side down, cover with greaseproof paper and then flatten with a meat mallet.

8 Twist the legs inwards and push them through the holes in the breasts.

9 Repeat with each poussin.

**10** Rub the poussins with the salt and spread the flesh sides evenly with half the yoghurt.

**11** Melt 2 oz (50g) of the butter in a large frying pan, add two poussins skin side down, place a heavy weight on top and cook over a moderate heat for 8 to 10 minutes.

**12** Turn the poussins over, spread with half the remaining yoghurt, weigh down and fry for a further 10 minutes until golden brown, but do not burn.

**13** Repeat with the two remaining poussins, while keeping the first two warm.

**14** Meanwhile melt the remaining 1 oz (25g) butter in a saucepan and sauté the tomatoes, aubergine, garlic and cinnamon until soft.

**15** Serve one poussin per person accompanied by some of the cooked vegetables and the *tkemali* sauce.

### DAMI GHALEBI BA MORGH
*Rice with chicken and dried fruit*

This Iranian dish is very decorative as well as delicious. Traditionally it is cooked in a mould and then inverted on to a serving platter to show a golden brown crust. However it can be layered in a casserole and baked in the oven or steamed in a saucepan over a low heat.

Salads and yoghurt drinks make ideal accompaniments.

*4 large prunes, stoned*
*8 dates, stoned*
*8 dried apricots*
*8 dried peaches (optional)*
*12 oz (350g) long-grained rice, washed thoroughly under cold running water and drained*
*2 teaspoons salt*
*4 chicken breasts, washed and dried*
*1 onion, thinly sliced*

*¼ pint (150ml) chicken stock or water*
*1 teaspoon salt*
*½ teaspoon black pepper*
*4 oz (100g) butter, melted*
*½ teaspoon saffron*
*¼ pint (150ml) yoghurt*
*2 oz (50g) chopped walnuts*
*2 oz (50g) raisins*

**1** Cut the prunes, dates, apricots and peaches into small pieces, place in a bowl of cold water and set aside.

**2** Place 1½ pints (1l) water and 2 teaspoons salt in a large saucepan and bring to the boil.

**3** Add the rice and simmer for about 20 minutes or until all the water has been absorbed.

**4** Meanwhile place the chicken breasts in a large saucepan with the onion, stock, salt and pepper.

**5** Cover and simmer for about 30 minutes, or until tender, turning occasionally.

**6** Cool the chicken and remove and discard the bones. Reserve the stock.

**7** Drain the dried fruit.

**8** In a small bowl mix together 2 oz (50g) melted butter, the saffron, the yoghurt and 1 cup of the cooked rice.

**9** If using a mould, grease it first and then coat its entire surface with this mixture. Over this mixture arrange first a layer of plain rice, then some dried fruit, some chicken pieces, some of the chopped walnuts and raisins and 1 or 2 teaspoons of the stock. Continue alternating layers until the mould is full, ending with a layer of rice.

**10** Mix the remaining melted butter and chicken stock together and pour over the top layer of rice.

**11** Bake in an oven preheated to 375°F (190°C, gas 5) for about 1 hour.

**12** To unmould, dip up to the rim in cold water for a couple of minutes and then invert on to a large serving dish.

**13** If you are using a casserole or saucepan then first spread the butter, saffron, yoghurt and rice mixture over the base and then alternate the ingredients as described above in 9 and 10.

**14** If using an ovenproof casserole, bake as for 11.

**15** If using a saucepan, place it over a low heat, wrap the lid in a tea-towel and place firmly on the pan. Steam for between 30 and 45 minutes.

## SOURYANI CHICKEN
### *Assyrian chicken with yoghurt*

Assyrians – what is left of that mighty nation – still survive in parts of the Middle East and though now ignored and forgotten by others, they retain their age-old culture and customs. I was given this recipe by an Assyrian friend from Baghdad. It is a very old recipe, although it has, no doubt, been extensively modernized with the passing of time.

| | |
|---|---|
| *1 roasting chicken (about 3 lb,* | *1 pint (600ml) chicken stock* |
| *1½kg), cut into 8 serving pieces* | *1 teaspoon salt* |
| *4 tablespoons butter or ghee* | *½ teaspoon black pepper* |
| *1 onion, finely chopped* | *2 tablespoons ground almonds* |
| *1 green pepper, finely sliced* | *½ pint (300ml) yoghurt* |
| *2 tablespoons* sumak *powder* | *1 teaspoon cayenne pepper* |
| *(see p. 198)* | *1 teaspoon ground cumin* |

**1** Melt the butter or ghee in a large saucepan and cook the chicken pieces until golden brown on all sides.

**2** Remove the chicken pieces from the pan to a large plate and keep warm.

**3** Add to the pan the onion and green pepper and sauté for a few minutes until the onion is soft and translucent. Add the stock, *sumak*, salt and pepper.

**4** Return the chicken pieces to the saucepan, cover, lower the heat and simmer for 40 to 60 minutes until the chicken is tender.

**5** Transfer the chicken pieces to a serving dish and keep warm.

**6** Add a few tablespoons of water to the ground almonds, stir to a smooth paste, add to the juices in the pan and bring to the boil, stirring all the time.

**7** Turn off the heat and add the yoghurt to the sauce, stirring all the time.

**8** Pour the sauce over the chicken and garnish with the cayenne pepper and cumin.

**9** Serve with an accompaniment of a rice or *burghul* pilav.


## NOUROV JUD
### *Chicken with pomegranates*

This is one of my family's specialities. It is simple and economical to make and looks stunning on the dinner table when decorated with the red pomegranate seeds. It is also very tasty!

| | |
|---|---|
| *1 chicken (about 3 lb, 1½kg)* | *1 onion, thinly sliced* |
| *2 oz (50g) butter* | *½ pint (300ml) chicken stock* |

1 teaspoon salt
½ teaspoon black pepper
½ teaspoon ground cumin
the seeds from 2 pomegranates

1 pint (600ml) yoghurt stabilized
with 1 egg or 1 tablespoon plain
flour

1  Wash and dry the chicken and cut into eight serving pieces.

2  Melt the butter in a large saucepan and sauté the onion until golden brown.

3  Add the chicken pieces, stock, salt, pepper and cumin, and bring to the boil.

4  Cover and simmer for about 45 minutes or until tender, turning occasionally.

5  When ready to serve, remove from the heat and spoon a few tablespoons of the hot sauce into the yoghurt.

6  Gently stir the yoghurt into the saucepan and just heat through but do not boil.

7  Arrange the chicken joints in a serving dish, pour the sauce over the top and then sprinkle the red pomegranate seeds all over it.

## MURGH TIKKA
### Skewered chicken

An easy way to cook chicken. It is a must in all Indian restaurants, and is traditionally served with an onion and tomato salad and chapatis.

2 lb (1kg) chicken joints, breasts or
  thighs
1 onion, roughly chopped
2 cloves garlic, roughly chopped
4 teaspoons finely chopped fresh
  ginger
juice of 1 large lemon

½ pint (300ml) yoghurt
2 teaspoons ground coriander
½ teaspoon ground cumin
2 teaspoons salt
3 tablespoons chopped fresh
  coriander or mint leaves

1  Remove the bones and skin from the joints.

2  Cut the chicken flesh into 1 in (3cm) pieces.

3  In a liquidizer blend the onion, garlic, ginger and lemon juice until smooth.

4  Empty this paste into a large bowl, add the yoghurt, coriander, cumin and salt, and mix well.

**5** Add the chicken pieces, turn until well coated and leave to marinate at room temperature for a few hours or in the refrigerator overnight.

**6** Thread the pieces of meat on to skewers and cook over charcoal or under the grill for 10 to 12 minutes, turning frequently.

**7** Serve immediately sprinkled with the chopped leaves and with a rice pilav of your choice or with chapatis.

## KINOV HAV
### *'Drunken chicken'*

What a wonderful description! I need add no more. Boiled or roast potatoes or a rice or *burghul* pilav make good accompaniments.

*1 chicken (about 3 lb, 1½kg)*
*seasoned flour – you can vary the ingredients, but basically they are: 2 oz (50g) flour, ½ teaspoon black pepper, ½ teaspoon marjoram, 1 teaspoon salt, ½ teaspoon fenugreek*

*2 oz (50g) butter*
*¼ pint (150ml) brandy*
*1 pint (600ml) yoghurt stabilized with 2 eggs*
*2 teaspoons paprika*
*a few sprigs of parsley*

**1** Clean, wash, dry and cut the chicken into eight serving pieces.

**2** Mix the seasoned flour on a large plate and roll the chicken pieces in it.

**3** Melt the butter in a large ovenproof casserole.

**4** Add the chicken and brown on all sides.

**5** Add the brandy and cover.

**6** Cook in the middle of the oven at 350°F (180°C, gas 4) for about 1 hour or until the chicken is tender. Baste regularly with the juices. If you like a crisp skin then remove the cover of the dish for the last 10 to 15 minutes.

**7** Pour in the stabilized yoghurt and cook over a low heat for a further 5 minutes.

**8** Spoon into a serving dish, pour the sauce over the top and sprinkle with the paprika.

**9** Serve immediately, garnished with the parsley.

## TANDOORI MURGH
### *Chicken tandoori*

Tandoori chicken is a north Indian dish, spread throughout the world in the last few years by countless Tandoori restaurants. Traditionally, the chicken is cooked in a *tandoor* (similar to the Turkish *tandir* and the Armenian *tonir*) – a cylindrical clay oven still popular in the remote villages of the Caucasus, Iran and Turkey, as well as India.

In a modern kitchen Tandoori chicken can be cooked in the oven or over charcoal.

1 chicken, about 3 lb (1½kg), skin removed
1 teaspoon cayenne pepper
2 tablespoons lemon juice
salt and pepper to taste

MARINADE
3–4 in (8–10cm) piece fresh ginger, peeled and chopped

4 cloves garlic, crushed
2 teaspoons whole coriander seeds
1 tablespoon cumin powder
2 tablespoons lemon juice
3 tablespoons yoghurt
1 tablespoon cayenne pepper
1 teaspoon red vegetable colouring
3 tablespoons ghee or butter, melted

1  Wash the chicken thoroughly and dry with kitchen paper.

2  In a small bowl mix the cayenne pepper, lemon juice, salt and black pepper together and rub the mixture all over the chicken.

3  Set aside for 45 minutes.

4  Meanwhile make the marinade by mixing all the ingredients together in a large bowl.

5  Place the chicken in the bowl and coat generously with the marinade.

6  Cover and refrigerate for 12 to 18 hours.

7  Remove the chicken, drain and thread whole on to a large skewer. If you find it easier, cut it in half and thread the halves on to two skewers. (In this case the cooking time will be 30 to 45 minutes.)

8  Cook over a charcoal grill, turning and basting regularly with the marinade so that it does not burn. Or roast it in the oven at 350°F (180°C, gas 4). Cook for 1 to 1½ hours or until cooked through. (Test by sticking the point of a sharp knife into the thigh.)

9  Serve immediately on a large platter garnished with thinly sliced onions, tomatoes and chopped chilli peppers, all dressed with lemon juice.

10  Accompany with chapatis or *naan* bread.

## MURGI DAHI
*Chicken in a yoghurt-curry sauce*

Let me be honest and say that this is my favourite dish from the Indian subcontinent.

Serve with bread or a rice pilav.

*8 chicken pieces, skinned*
*½ pint (300ml) yoghurt*
*1 onion, roughly chopped*
*3 cloves garlic*
*2 green chillies*
*1½ in (4cm) piece fresh root ginger, peeled and chopped*
*1 red or green pepper, seeded and coarsely chopped*
*1 teaspoon cumin seeds*
*1 teaspoon paprika*
*1 teaspoon salt*
*1½ oz (40g) ghee or butter*
*2 tablespoons finely chopped coriander leaves*
*juice of ¼ lemon*
*fresh coriander or mint leaves for garnish*

**1** Prick the chicken pieces all over with a fork, place in a bowl and set aside.

**2** In a liquidizer blend the yoghurt, onion, garlic, chillies, ginger, cumin seeds, pepper, paprika and salt together until the mixture is smooth.

**3** Pour this marinade over the chicken pieces and use your fingers to rub it in well.

**4** Cover the bowl and set aside for 4 hours.

**5** Put the chicken pieces and marinade into a large saucepan.

**6** Bring to the boil over a moderate heat and when it has been bubbling for about 2 minutes lower the heat and cook, stirring frequently, for 35 to 40 minutes or until it is tender and the sauce is very thick.

**7** Remove the pan from the heat.

**8** Melt the butter in a large frying pan and add the chicken pieces.

**9** Reduce the heat and fry the chicken pieces very gently, turning them over in the butter so that they are well coated, for 3 minutes.

**10** Spoon the sauce and the scrapings left in the saucepan over the chicken.

**11** Sprinkle the chopped coriander leaves and lemon juice over the chicken, cover and cook for a further 5 minutes.

**12** Spoon the chicken and sauce on to a preheated dish and serve immediately, garnished with the coriander or mint leaves.

## KHORSHT-E MAST
### Chicken in an orange and yoghurt sauce

This Iranian dish can also be prepared with lamb – use 2 lb (1kg) lean lamb, boned and cut into 1½ in (4cm) pieces. The attractive creamy sauce has a delicate, tangy flavour.

Serve with a plain rice pilau.

1 chicken, about 3 lb (1½kg) cut into 8 pieces
1 oz (25g) butter
2 small onions, thinly sliced
1 pint (600ml) chicken stock
½ teaspoon black pepper

1 teaspoon salt
½ teaspoon saffron
skin of 1 orange pared very thinly so that there is no white pith
¾ pint (450ml) yoghurt, stabilized with 1 egg

**1** In a large heavy-based saucepan or casserole melt the butter and sauté the onions until they are golden brown.

**2** Stir in the stock, salt, pepper and saffron.

**3** Add the chicken pieces, turn in the stock, cover and simmer for about an hour or until tender. Turn the pieces at least once so that they are cooked all over.

**4** Stir in the thinly sliced orange peel and simmer, uncovered, for a further 20 minutes.

**5** Pour the stabilized yoghurt into a small bowl and stir in a few tablespoons of the hot stock.

**6** Now slowly stir the yoghurt mixture into the hot stock.

**7** Gently simmer for a further 5 to 10 minutes and remove from the heat.

**8** Serve in a deep bowl accompanied by the rice.


## DAJAJ MAHSHI
### Stuffed chicken marinated in yoghurt

This dish is popular in one form or another throughout Turkey, Syria, Lebanon, Armenia and Jordan. Ideal with fresh salads and a drink of *tan*.

1 (about 3–4 lb, 1½–2kg) roasting chicken (with giblets)
2 oz (50g) butter
1 small onion, finely chopped

2 tablespoons pine kernels – if you cannot find them or cannot afford them use split almonds instead
6 oz (175g) rice, washed thoroughly

under cold running water
1 tablespoon raisins
4 teaspoons salt
1 teaspoon black pepper

½ cinnamon stick
1 oz (25g) butter, melted
2 tablespoons chopped parsley
½ pint (300ml) yoghurt

**1** Remove giblets from the chicken, wash the liver and heart, and chop finely.

**2** Melt the butter in a saucepan, add the onion and sauté until golden brown.

**3** Add the chopped giblets and pine kernels and cook for 2 to 3 minutes.

**4** Stir in the rice and cook for about 5 minutes, turning frequently so that all the grains are coated with butter.

**5** Add ¾ pint (450ml) water, and the raisins, 2 teaspoons of the salt, ½ teaspoon of the black pepper and the cinnamon stick.

**6** Bring to the boil, lower the heat and simmer until the liquid has been completely absorbed.

**7** Remove from the heat, discard the cinnamon stick and stir in the melted butter and parsley.

**8** Wash the chicken and pat dry with kitchen paper.

**9** Fill the cavity with the rice stuffing. If there is any remaining, set it aside to serve later with the chicken.

**10** Close the opening.

**11** Mix the remaining salt and black pepper with the yoghurt.

**12** Place the chicken in a bowl, pour the yoghurt over the top and rub it into the chicken, making sure that all parts are covered.

**13** Cover and leave in the refrigerator overnight, turning occasionally.

**14** Preheat oven to 350°F (180°C, gas 4) and roast, covered, for about 2½ hours until very tender and golden brown. Remove the lid for the last 30 minutes.

**15** Transfer the chicken to a serving dish and spoon the stuffing into a separate dish, together with the remaining rice, which you have heated through.

## PAPRIKAS CSIRKE
### *Chicken paprika with yoghurt*

This is a paprika dish from Hungary, flavoured with the magnificent peppers of the region. The sauce is traditionally made with a mixture of cream and soured cream, but yoghurt is an excellent substitute.

It is usually accompanied by a bowl of small pasta shells.

*1 chicken (about 3 lb, 1½kg), cut into 6 joints*
*2 oz (50g) lard*
*1 onion, finely chopped*
*2 tablespoons paprika*
*2 teaspoons salt*
*1 green pepper, cut into strips*

*3 tomatoes, blanched, peeled, seeded and chopped*
*¼ pint (150ml) chicken stock*
*½ pint (300ml) yoghurt stabilized with 1 egg or 1 tablespoon plain flour*

**1** Wash and dry the chicken joints.

**2** Melt the lard in a large, heavy-based saucepan or casserole.

**3** Add the pieces of chicken and fry on both sides until golden brown, then place on a plate.

**4** Add the onion to the remaining lard, cover and cook very gently for about 20 minutes until soft and golden.

**5** Stir in the paprika, salt, green pepper and chopped tomatoes.

**6** Return the chicken joints and pour in the stock.

**7** Turn the joints to ensure they are coated with the vegetables and liquid. The joints should be at least half covered with liquid. If not add a little more.

**8** Cover and simmer gently for ¾ to 1 hour until the chicken is tender.

**9** Remove the joints to a serving dish and keep warm.

**10** Pour the stabilized yoghurt into a bowl and stir in 3 to 4 tablespoons of the paprika sauce.

**11** Stir the yoghurt mixture into the casserole, heat through, taste and adjust seasoning if necessary.

**12** Pour the sauce over the chicken joints and serve immediately.

## PEČENA DIVLJA PLORKA
*Roast duck with yoghurt sauce*

This Yugoslav recipe normally uses wild duck, but this is not readily available here and so I suggest using ordinary duck or goose.

*1 oz (25g) butter*
*2 onions, sliced*
*1 duck or goose – about 5 lb (2½kg)*
*  – cleaned, washed and dried*
*4 tablespoons oil*
*juice of 1 lemon*
*1 teaspoon salt*

*4–5 rashers streaky bacon*
*1 teaspoon cumin*
*1 bay leaf*
*salt and pepper to taste*
*1 pint (600ml) yoghurt stabilized*
*   with 1 egg*

**1** Melt the butter in a saucepan and sauté the onions until soft.

**2** Meanwhile prick the skin of the bird in several places, then mix the oil, lemon juice and salt together and rub the mixture into the skin.

**3** Place the bacon rashers over the breast of the bird.

**4** When the onions are tender, add ½ pint (300ml) water, and the cumin, bay leaf, salt and pepper to taste and bring to the boil.

**5** Pour the mixture into the roasting tin and then place the bird in the centre.

**6** Roast in a moderate oven (350°F, 180°C, gas 4) for about 2 hours or until tender. Baste frequently with the sauce in the pan.

**7** When cooked remove the bird, carve and keep the meat warm while you complete the sauce.

**8** Add the yoghurt to the sauce and heat through but do not boil.

**9** Strain the sauce and pour it over the duck.

**10** Serve immediately.

# FISH

### RASCIAN CARP
*Carp with potatoes and yoghurt*

This is an adaptation of a famous Hungarian recipe.
Accompany with a simple cucumber and tomato salad.

*1 whole carp, 5–6 lb (2½–3kg) in weight*
*1 teaspoon salt*
*1 teaspoon paprika*
*4 oz (100g) bacon rashers, cut into 2–3 in (5–8cm) strips*
*2 lb (1kg) potatoes*
*1 onion, sliced*

*5–6 green paprikas; if you cannot get them then use 2 green peppers, thinly sliced*
*3 large tomatoes, sliced*
*3 oz (75g) butter, melted*
*¾ pint (450ml) yoghurt stabilized with 1 egg or 1 tablespoon plain flour*

1 Scale, remove any entrails and wash the fish under cold running water.

2 With a sharp knife split it into two and then cut into ½ lb (200g) pieces and score them.

3 Sprinkle with the salt and paprika.

4 Put the thin slices of bacon into the incisions.

5 Meanwhile peel, wash and cut the potatoes into thick slices.

6 Parboil in slightly salted water for 5 minutes.

7 Now butter a large ovenproof dish and cover the bottom with the potatoes.

8 Put the fish into the dish and cover with sliced onion, paprikas or green peppers and tomatoes.

9 Baste with the melted butter and put the dish into an oven preheated to 350°F (180°C, gas 4).

10 When half cooked – after about 20 minutes – remove the dish from

the oven and pour the stabilized yoghurt over the fish, return to the oven and continue cooking until both the fish and the potatoes are ready.

## YOGURTLU USKUMRU DOLMASI
### *Mackerel stuffed with pine kernels and currants*

This is a slight variation on the great Turkish classic, *uskumru dolmasi* – stuffed mackerel. Traditionalists may object, but I do think the yoghurt adds a subtle flavour to what is already a great dish.

*4 whole mackerel, about 12 oz (350g) each*
*salt*
*5 tablespoons olive oil*
*1 onion, finely chopped*
*2 oz (50g) pine kernels*
*1 oz (25g) fresh breadcrumbs*
*½ teaspoon coriander seeds*
*½ teaspoon ground cinnamon*
*black pepper to taste*

*3 tablespoons finely chopped parsley*
*2 oz (50g) currants, soaked for 1 hour in warm water*
*3 tablespoons fresh dill or 3 teaspoons dried dillweed*
*4 tomatoes, sliced*
*½ pint (300ml) yoghurt stabilized with 1 tablespoon plain flour*
*lemon wedges for garnish*

1 First prepare the fish for stuffing:
   (*a*) Cut off the fins with scissors.
   (*b*) Break the backbone at the base of the tail by bending the tail sharply forwards over the body.
   (*c*) Roll the fish backwards and forwards under the palms of your hands on a flat surface for a few minutes to loosen the backbone.
   (*d*) Turn the fish over on to its back and cut down through the throat just behind the gills leaving the head attached by a piece of skin about ½ in (1cm) wide.
   (*e*) Scoop out and discard the entrails.
   (*f*) Wash the fish inside and out.
   (*g*) Hold the body tightly with one hand and with the other pull out the backbone.
   (*h*) Starting from the tail gently press the fish with your thumbs to push out as much of the flesh as possible, while keeping the

skin intact and the head attached so that the fish can be easily re-assembled.

2  Place the fish in a large pan, sprinkle with some salt, completely cover with cold water and set aside for 30 minutes.

3  Place fish meat in sieve, wash under cold running water, drain, pat dry with kitchen paper and set aside.

4  Make the stuffing by heating 4 tablespoons of olive oil in a large pan.

5  Add the onion and sauté until soft.

6  Stir in the pine kernels and cook until lightly browned.

7  Add the fish meat, breadcrumbs, coriander, cinnamon, 1 teaspoon of salt and black pepper to taste.

8  Stir frequently and cook for 5 minutes.

9  Remove from the heat and stir in the parsley, currants and dill, and leave to cool.

10  Preheat oven to 400°F (200°C, gas 6).

11  Brush the bottom and sides of a large, shallow ovenproof dish with 1 tablespoon of oil.

12  Wash the fish under cold running water and pat dry, inside and out, with kitchen paper.

13  Put a quarter of the stuffing into each fish.

14  Close the openings with needle and thread or small skewers.

15  Arrange the mackerel side by side in the dish.

16  Arrange the tomato slices along the length of each fish.

17  Blend ¼ pint (150ml) water with the stabilized yoghurt and pour into the dish.

18  Heat the dish on top of the stove until the sauce is about to boil and then transfer to the oven.

19  Bake for about 30 minutes or until the fish feels firm to the touch.

20  Serve immediately, garnished with the lemon wedges.

### PRAWN PATHIA
*Curried prawns in yoghurt*

A popular Indian dish which makes use of prawns and a yoghurt-based curry sauce. It has a delicate flavour and is excellent on a bed of boiled rice or eaten with *naan* or *parathas*.

4 oz (100g) ghee or butter
2 onions, finely chopped
3 oz (75g) shredded coconut, coarse
 variety
1 teaspoon chilli powder
1 teaspoon paprika
2 in (5cm) stick cinnamon
3 bay leaves

1½ teaspoons garam masala
 (see p. 197)
1 tablespoon fenugreek
1 teaspoon ground ginger
2 tablespoons tomato purée
¾ pint (450ml) stabilized yoghurt
1 lb (½kg) frozen prawns, thawed,
 or use fresh prawns

**1** In a large saucepan melt the ghee or butter and fry the onions until golden brown.

**2** Add the coconut and cook until brown.

**3** Add the chilli powder, paprika, cinnamon, bay leaves, *garam masala*, fenugreek and ginger and stir well.

**4** Stir in the tomato purée and yoghurt.

**5** Bring to the boil and immediately lower the heat.

**6** Add the prawns and stir well.

**7** Cover the pan and simmer slowly, stirring frequently to prevent sticking, for 30 minutes, or until the prawns are well cooked and the sauce is thick.

### SOM BALIGI
*Salmon with yoghurt*

This is an adaptation of a popular Turkish dish. Salmon is highly prized among the Turks and is reserved for special occasions. The dish is found in most good Istanbul and Ismir restaurants.

4 salmon steaks
1 small carrot, grated
1 small onion, chopped
1 stick celery, chopped
2 bay leaves
1 clove garlic, chopped
2 cloves
4 peppercorns

8 oz (200g) cooked spinach, chopped
2 tablespoons plain flour
½ pint (300ml) yoghurt
1½ teaspoons salt
½ teaspoon nutmeg
1 oz (25g) breadcrumbs
2 oz (50g) haloumi or Parmesan
 cheese, grated

**1** Place the salmon steaks in a large, deep saucepan and add sufficient boiling water to cover.

**2** Add the carrot, onion, celery, bay leaves, garlic, cloves and peppercorns.

**3** Simmer until the fish can easily be separated from the bone.

**4** Remove the fish steaks with a slotted spoon to a plate and keep hot.

**5** Raise the heat and boil vigorously until the stock has been reduced to ¾–1 pint (450–600ml) and then strain, retaining the stock and discarding the vegetables.

**6** Meanwhile prepare the spinach and keep it warm.

**7** Put the flour into a small bowl, add 3–4 tablespoons of the hot stock and stir until smooth.

**8** Add this to the remaining stock and heat through, stirring constantly until the sauce thickens. Simmer very gently for 5 to 10 minutes.

**9** Remove the sauce from the heat and stir in the yoghurt, salt and nutmeg.

**10** Arrange the spinach on a heatproof serving dish and arrange the fish steaks on it.

**11** Pour the sauce over the top.

**12** Sprinkle with the breadcrumbs and cheese and place under a hot grill for 3 to 5 minutes until golden brown.

**13** Serve immediately.

## MAREMKHODOV TZOOK
*Trout with yoghurt and marjoram*

I was given this recipe by a friend who hails from Kurdistan. It is simple to make, attractive to look at and has a subtle creamy flavour. Instead of trout you can use red or grey mullet.

*Kaymak* is the thick cream popular in the Middle East which is usually made from sheep's milk. Use double cream or, if you can get it, clotted cream.

Garnish with spring onions and fresh tarragon leaves and serve with sweet boiled potatoes or sautéed potatoes.

4 trout
1 oz (25g) ghee or butter, melted
1 tablespoon sweet marjoram
1 teaspoon salt
½ teaspoon black pepper
¼ pint (150ml) yoghurt

¼ pint (150ml) kaymak, *double cream or clotted cream*
1 tablespoon plain flour
2 limes or lemons, cut into wedges, to garnish

1  Ask your fishmonger to remove the entrails and clean out the fish.

2  Wash the fish under cold running water and dry with kitchen paper.

3  Place the fish side by side in a lightly buttered baking dish.

4  Brush the melted ghee or butter over the fish and then sprinkle with the marjoram, salt and pepper.

5  Mix the yoghurt and cream together in a bowl and then stir in the flour.

6  Pour this mixture over the fish and bake in an oven preheated to 350°F (180°C, gas 4) for 30 to 45 minutes or until the fish are well cooked.

7  Serve garnished with the lime or lemon wedges, spring onions and tarragon leaves.

## MADZNOV ISHKAN
### Stuffed trout with almond and yoghurt sauce

This is traditionally made with the trout called *Ishkan*–'Prince of Trouts' – found only in Lake Sevan in Armenia. Brown or rainbow trout would be suitable substitutes.

4 trout
cooking oil or butter

STUFFING
¼ lb (100g) ground almonds
juice of 2 lemons
about ¼ pint (150ml) yoghurt
1 teaspoon salt
1 teaspoon black pepper
1 teaspoon cumin

SAUCE
¼ lb (100g) ground almonds
1 glass white wine
about ¼ pint (150ml) yoghurt, stabilized
salt and black pepper to taste
a few thin slices green pepper

GARNISH
lemon wedges

**1** Have your fishmonger clean out the fish, but do not have the heads or tails cut off.

**2** Mix the ingredients for the stuffing together in a bowl.

**3** Add sufficient yoghurt to produce a thick paste.

**4** Divide the mixture into four and fill each trout.

**5** Heat the butter or oil in a large baking dish.

**6** Place the fish in the dish, brush with a little oil and cook in an oven preheated to 400°F (200°C, gas 6) for 20 to 30 minutes.

**7** Meanwhile prepare the sauce in a small saucepan. Mix the almonds with the wine and yoghurt.

**8** Season with the salt and pepper.

**9** Add sufficient water to make the consistency that you prefer.

**10** Bring to the boil and then simmer gently for about 10 minutes.

**11** Just before serving add the green pepper. Do not cook for more than a minute or two or it will lose its crispness and colour.

**12** When the fish are cooked, arrange them on a large dish with the lemon wedges and serve with the sauce.

## FISH CURRY

The finest fish dishes on the Indian subcontinent originate in Bangladesh, which has an abundance of fish of all kinds.

*1 lb (½kg) fish, e.g. tuna, bonito or halibut*
*1 teaspoon turmeric*
*1 teaspoon salt*
*½ teaspoon root ginger, grated*
*2 fresh green chilli peppers*
*2 red chillies, if available, or 2 teaspoons chilli powder*

*½ pint (300ml) stabilized yoghurt*
*4 tablespoons mustard oil if available – otherwise use vegetable oil*
*2 oz (50g) ghee or butter*
*1 onion, finely chopped*
*2 bay leaves*
*1½ teaspoons curry powder*

**1** Clean, scale and wash the fish. Cut into ten to twelve pieces.

**2** Mix the turmeric, salt and grated ginger together.

**3** Rub the mixture into the fish.

**4** Seed the chillies and finely slice them.

**5** Pour the yoghurt into a bowl and stir in the chillies or chilli powder.

**6** Meanwhile heat the mustard or vegetable oil in a large saucepan, add the ghee or butter and onion, and sauté until soft and lightly browned.

**7** Add the yoghurt mixture, bay leaves and curry powder, stir and cook gently for a few minutes.

**8** Add the fish pieces and turn until they are well coated and then simmer for about 20 minutes or until the fish flakes easily and the sauce has thickened.

**9** Serve on a bed of saffron rice pilav.

## PLAICE CASSEROLE

This is a simple, relatively cheap recipe. I have chosen plaice because I like its delicate taste, but there is no reason why you should not use flounder, brill or turbot instead. Accompany it with a cooked vegetable of your choice and boiled or roast potatoes.

| | |
|---|---|
| 1 whole plaice (about 1–1½ lb, ½–¾kg), or any other flat fish | ½ teaspoon oregano |
| ½ pint (300ml) yoghurt | 1 teaspoon salt |
| 1 egg yolk, well beaten | a pinch of paprika |
| 3 tablespoons dry white wine | 2–3 bay leaves |
| 1½ tablespoons lemon juice | 2 oz (50g) breadcrumbs |
| | 2 tablespoons finely chopped parsley |

**1** Get the fishmonger to clean out the fish for you. If he won't do it without filleting it, then do it yourself. Make a semicircular slit just behind the head on the dark skin side. The cavity which opens here contains the entrails. Scrape these out, wash the fish thoroughly and cut off the fins.

**2** Arrange the fish in a buttered baking dish.

**3** Pour the yoghurt into a bowl, add the egg yolk, wine, lemon juice, oregano, salt and paprika, and beat lightly.

**4** Pour this mixture over the fish and add the bay leaves.

**5** Sprinkle the breadcrumbs over the top and bake for 50 minutes or so in an oven preheated to 375°F (190°C, gas 5).

**6** Just before serving garnish with the parsley.

## BULGARIAN FISH WITH YOGHURT

This is a typically Balkan dish with paprika, grated cheese, mushrooms, oregano and yoghurt. It is popular throughout Eastern Europe – the Romanians and Hungarians use soured cream, while the Bulgarians prefer yoghurt.

2 lb (1kg) halibut
flour
salt and pepper
2 oz (50g) butter, melted
2 hard-boiled eggs, shelled and sliced
2 oz (50g) mushrooms, washed,
  dried and thinly sliced

2 tablespoons paprika
2 oz (50g) grated cheese e.g.
  Parmesan, Cheddar or haloumi –
  I prefer the latter
½ pint (300ml) yoghurt stabilized
  with 1 tablespoon plain flour

**1** Wash the fish, dry thoroughly and cut into 2 in (5cm) pieces, discarding the bones.

**2** Dust with flour and sprinkle with salt and pepper.

**3** Pour the butter into a baking dish and arrange the fish in the dish.

**4** Arrange the egg slices and mushrooms over the fish.

**5** Sprinkle with the paprika.

**6** Mix the cheese and yoghurt and spoon over the fish, egg and mushrooms.

**7** Bake in the centre of an oven preheated to 350°F (180°C, gas 4) for about 30 minutes or until the fish flakes easily with a fork.

**8** Serve accompanied by a light green salad and boiled potatoes.

## TIRANA FISH STEW

*Albanian fish stew*

Another Balkan speciality, this time from Albania. Serve on a bed of rice pilav or boiled noodles.

3 tablespoons olive oil
1 onion, thinly sliced
1 clove garlic, finely chopped
2 tablespoons tomato purée
1 glass dry white wine
6 potatoes, peeled and thinly sliced
2 bay leaves
1 teaspoon salt

½ teaspoon black pepper
¼ teaspoon dried basil
¼ teaspoon cayenne pepper
1½ lb (750g) white fish e.g. halibut,
  cut into 1–1½ in (3–4cm) pieces
½ pint (300ml) yoghurt, stabilized
  with 1 egg
2 tablespoons finely chopped parsley

1 Heat the oil in a large saucepan and sauté the onion and garlic until soft and translucent.

2 Add the tomato purée and stir well.

3 Add 1 pint (600ml) water, with the wine, potatoes, bay leaves, salt, black pepper, basil and cayenne pepper, and mix well.

4 Cover the pan and cook on a medium heat for 10 to 12 minutes.

5 Add the fish pieces and cook for a further 15 to 20 minutes or until the potatoes and fish are tender.

6 Mix in the yoghurt and parsley and heat through but do not boil; serve.

## TZAVAROV LETZONADZE TZOOK
### *Fish stuffed with burghul*

This Caucasian dish is traditionally made with bream, but any white fish will do. It is usually stuffed with *kasha* (buckwheat), but I think *tzavar* (*burghul*) is far better. The Circassians and Georgians use soured cream instead of yoghurt.

*2–3 lb (1–1½kg) whole white fish,*
   *e.g. bream, halibut, cod, etc.*
*3 oz (75g) butter*
*2 onions, finely chopped*
*12 oz (350g) coarse* burghul
*3 hard-boiled eggs, shelled and*
   *coarsely chopped*
*2 tablespoons finely chopped parsley*

*2 tablespoons fresh dill*
   *or 2 teaspoons dried dillweed*
*1 teaspoon salt*
*½ teaspoon black pepper*
*½ pint (300ml) yoghurt stabilized*
   *with 1 tablespoon plain flour*
*1 teaspoon* sumak *(see p. 198)*

1 Remove the entrails and wash the fish under cold running water; dry thoroughly with kitchen paper.

2 In a large saucepan melt 2 oz (50g) of the butter and sauté the onions until soft.

3 Add the *burghul*, chopped eggs, parsley, dill, salt, and pepper. Mix thoroughly and cook gently for 4 to 5 minutes.

4 Sprinkle the cavity of the fish with a little salt and spoon the *burghul* mixture into the cavity. Do not press too hard as the *burghul* will expand during cooking.

5 Arrange the fish in a large buttered baking dish.

6 Dot little knobs of the remaining butter over the fish.

**7** Bake in the centre of the oven preheated to 400°F (200°C, gas 6) for 10 to 15 minutes, or until the fish is almost tender.

**8** Remove the baking dish, pour the yoghurt over the fish and return it to the centre of the oven.

**9** Cook for a further 5 to 8 minutes.

**10** Remove from the oven and sprinkle with the *sumak* powder.

**11** Serve with *lavash* or pitta bread and a bowl of fresh herbs and vegetables such as sliced cucumbers and tomatoes.

## BARZ TZOOK
### Fish with walnuts

The translation of this name is 'simple fish' and that is just what it is – fish with yoghurt and herbs. It is popular throughout the Middle East, but especially in the Caucasus and northern Iran, where great use is made of fresh herbs. The 'crumble' topping makes this a very attractive dish when served.

*2 lb (1kg) white fish steaks, e.g. cod, halibut or swordfish*
*1 teaspoon salt*
*½ teaspoon black pepper*
*½ pint (300ml) yoghurt stabilized with 1 tablespoon plain flour*
*juice of 1 lemon*

*3–4 spring onions, finely chopped*
*2 oz (50g) breadcrumbs*
*2 oz (50g) chopped walnuts*
*1 oz (25g) butter, melted*
*2 tablespoons finely chopped parsley*
*1 tablespoon finely chopped fresh basil or 1 teaspoon dried basil*

**1** Wash the fish steaks and pat them dry on kitchen paper.

**2** Sprinkle both sides of the fish with salt and pepper to taste.

**3** Lightly butter a large shallow baking dish and arrange the fish steaks in the bottom.

**4** Mix the yoghurt with the lemon juice and the chopped spring onions and spoon over the fish.

**5** Now mix the breadcrumbs and the walnuts into the melted butter, together with the parsley and basil.

**6** Spread this mixture over the fish and cook in a moderate oven, 350°F (180°C, gas 4), for 30 to 40 minutes or until the fish steaks are easily flaked with a fork.

**7** This dish is traditionally served with side dishes of spring onions, radishes, dill, tarragon, etc.

## MACHCHI KEBAB

From India comes this skewered fish kebab marinated in all the regional spices. Traditionally cooked in a *tandoor*, it is also excellent when cooked over charcoal, or for convenience under the grill, though of course the flavour will not be the same. Serve with chapatis or pitta bread and an accompaniment of thinly sliced onions, green chillies and mint leaves dressed with lime juice.

2 lb (1kg) fish, e.g. snapper, hake or
   haddock, filleted

MARINADE
2 teaspoons fresh ginger, finely
   chopped
2 cloves garlic, finely chopped

2 teaspoons salt
1 teaspoon garam masala
juice of 2 lemons
½ pint (300ml) yoghurt
1 teaspoon chilli powder
3 teaspoons ground coriander
2 tablespoons plain flour

1  Wash the fish and dry with kitchen paper.

2  Cut the fish into 1 in (3cm) pieces.

3  Put all the marinade ingredients together in a large bowl and mix together thoroughly.

4  Add the fish cubes, toss them in the marinade and leave for 30 minutes at room temperature or for 1 hour, covered, in the refrigerator.

5  Thread the fish cubes on to skewers and cook over charcoal or under the grill for about 10 minutes, turning once or twice.

6  Do not overcook.

7  Remove from the fire and serve immediately.

## CAUCASIAN HAKE

This is a classic dish of the Caucasus and I understand that a very similar dish is extremely popular in the Balkans. It is a tasty fish casserole traditionally served with a side bowl of fresh herbs, e.g. tarragon, parsley, chives, spring onions, etc. Although there are potatoes in the dish I found that a few extra sautéed potatoes made an ideal accompaniment.

*4 fish steaks – preferably hake, but halibut or cod will do*
*1 lb (½kg) potatoes, peeled and cut crossways into ¼ in (½cm) slices*
*1 onion, thinly sliced*
*2 oz (50g) butter*
*3 tomatoes, thinly sliced*

*1 teaspoon salt*
*1 tablespoon* sumak *powder* *(see p. 198)*
*¾ pint (450ml) yoghurt*
*1 tablespoon flour*
*2 teaspoons paprika*

**1** Wash the steaks under cold running water and pat dry with kitchen paper.

**2** Lightly butter a large ovenproof dish and preheat oven to 325°F (160°C, gas 3).

**3** Arrange the slices of potato and onion in the dish and dot with the butter.

**4** Arrange the slices of tomato over the top and sprinkle with the salt and *sumak*.

**5** Cover and cook in the oven for 30 to 40 minutes.

**6** Remove from the oven and place the fish steaks on top of the vegetables.

**7** Mix the yoghurt, flour and paprika together with 2 or 3 tablespoons of the hot sauce and pour over the fish.

**8** Cover, return to the oven and cook for a further 45 minutes or until the fish is well cooked.

**9** Serve immediately.

# ACCOMPANIMENTS

## PLAIN RICE PILAV

When cooking rice, volume is more important than weight and the general rule is as follows: for the first teacup of rice (6 oz, 175g) use 2 teacups of liquid (475ml) and for every further teacup of rice use 1½ teacups of liquid (350ml). This recipe is a standard Middle Eastern one.

2 oz (50g) butter or ghee
9 oz (250g) long-grain rice, washed
   thoroughly under cold water and
   drained

1 teaspoon salt
1 pint (600ml) stock or water,
   boiling

**1** Melt the butter or ghee in a saucepan.

**2** Add the rice and fry for 2 to 3 minutes, stirring frequently.

**3** Stir in the salt and boiling stock or water.

**4** Allow the mixture to boil vigorously for about 3 minutes and then cover, lower the heat and simmer for 15 to 20 minutes or until the liquid has been absorbed.

**5** The grains should be tender and separate and there should be small holes in the surface of the pilav.

**6** Turn off the heat, remove the lid, cover the saucepan with a clean tea-towel, replace the lid and leave to 'rest' for 10 to 15 minutes.

**7** Gently fluff up the rice with a long-pronged fork, taking care not to break the grains, and serve.

## BURGHUL PILAV
### Cracked wheat pilav

A particular favourite of Armenians and Turks, burghul has, in recent years, appeared in the West. Burghul can be bought from many Middle Eastern and health food shops. When purchasing it to make a pilav make sure that you take the coarse or large-grained burghul. It makes an excellent pilav and is, perhaps, the cereal which goes best with yoghurt. It has a strong, earthy flavour and colour.

| | |
|---|---|
| *9 oz (250g) large-grained burghul* | *¾ pint (450ml) stock or water,* |
| *2 oz (50g) butter or ghee* | *boiling* |
| *1 oz (25g) vermicelli, broken into 1* | *1 teaspoon salt* |
| *in (2.5cm) pieces* | *½ teaspoon black pepper* |

**1** Put the burghul into a bowl or fine sieve and wash several times until the water runs clear. Leave to drain.

**2** Melt the butter or ghee in a saucepan.

**3** Add the vermicelli and fry until golden, stirring constantly.

**4** Add the burghul and fry for a further 2 or 3 minutes, stirring frequently.

**5** Add the boiling stock or water, salt and pepper, and stir well.

**6** Bring to the boil and boil vigorously for 3 minutes.

**7** Lower the heat and simmer for 8 to 10 minutes or until the water has been absorbed.

**8** Turn off the heat, cover the pan with a clean tea-towel, fit the lid over the top and leave to 'rest' for 10 to 15 minutes.

## PITTA
### *Arab bread*

Perhaps the most popular Middle Eastern bread in Europe. Pitta is Syrian by origin and was known by the ancient Assyrians and Babylonians who filled its pocket with vegetables or cooked meats – as is still the custom today.

You can purchase pittas from most continental stores, but if you wish to bake your own then try this recipe.

| | |
|---|---|
| TO MAKE EIGHT PITTAS | *1 teaspoon sugar* |
| *½ oz (15g) fresh yeast or ¼ oz* | *1 lb (450g) plain flour* |
| *(8g, 1 rounded teaspoon) dried* | *½ teaspoon salt* |
| *yeast* | *1 tablespoon oil (optional)* |

**1** Place the yeast and sugar in a small bowl, dissolve in a few tablespoons warm water and set aside in a warm place for about 10 minutes or until it begins to froth.

**2** Sift the flour and salt into a large bowl.

**3** Make a well in the centre and pour in the yeast mixture.

**4** Add enough warm water to make a firm, but not hard, dough, (about ½ pint, 300ml).

**5** Knead on a floured working top for 10 to 15 minutes or until the dough is soft and elastic.

**6** If you knead in a tablespoon of oil it will make a softer dough.

**7** Wash and dry the mixing bowl and lightly oil it.

**8** Roll the dough around the bowl until its surface is greased all over – this will prevent the dough going crusty and cracking while rising.

**9** Cover the dough with a damp cloth and set aside in a warm place for at least 2 hours until the dough has doubled in size.

**10** Transfer the dough to the working top, punch down and knead for a few minutes.

**11** Divide the mixture into eight pieces.

**12** Roll them between your palms until they are round and smooth.

**13** Lightly flour the working top and flatten each ball with the palm of your hand, or with a rolling pin, until it is about ¼in (½cm) thick and is as even and circular as possible.

**14** Dust the tops with flour and cover with a floured cloth.

**15** Leave to rise in a warm place for a further 20 to 30 minutes.

**16** Preheat the oven to 450–475°F (230–240°C, gas 8–9), putting in two large oiled baking sheets half-way through the heating period.

**17** When the oven is ready, slide the rounds of dough on to the hot baking sheets, damping the tops of the rounds to prevent them browning, and bake for 10 minutes.

**18** Do not open the oven door during this time, but after that it is safe to open it to see if the pittas have puffed up.

**19** Slide them on to wire racks as soon as you remove them from the oven.

**20** They should be soft and white with a pouch inside.

## LAVASH
*Thin crispy bread*

This is the bread of Armenia similar to *naan*. It often measures up to 2 ft (60cm) in diameter and is only ⅛ in (3mm) thick. Baked in a *tonir* (*tandoor*), it is always made in large quantities and then stacked and stored for winter use.

Lavash goes well with many dishes, but is particularly good with kebabs, roasts and salads.

> ½ oz (15g) fresh yeast or ¼ oz (8g) dried yeast
> 1 teaspoon sugar
> 1½ lb (680g) plain flour
> 1 teaspoon salt

**1** Place the yeast in a small bowl with the sugar, dissolve in ½ pint (300ml) warm water and set aside for about 10 minutes in a warm place until the mixture begins to froth.

**2** Sift the flour and salt into a large bowl.

**3** Make a well in the centre and slowly work in the yeast mixture and enough warm water to make a stiff dough.

**4** Knead on a floured surface for about 10 minutes until the dough is smooth and elastic.

**5** Place the ball of dough in a clean bowl, cover with a cloth and leave in a warm place for about 2 to 3 hours or until it has doubled in size.

**6** Transfer the dough to a floured surface, punch it down and knead again for a few minutes.

**7** Return to the bowl, cover and leave for a further 30 minutes.

**8** Flour the working surface again.

**9** Divide the dough into apple-sized balls. This amount of dough should make twelve to fifteen.

**10** With a long rolling pin roll out each ball into a thin sheet about 8–10 ins (20–25cm) in diameter.

**11** Sprinkle the working surface with flour now and again to prevent sticking.

**12** Line the bottom of the oven with foil and heat the oven to 400°F (200°C, gas 6).

**13** Place a sheet of dough on the foil and cook for about 3 minutes.

**14** Remove the cooked lavash and cover with a tea-towel while you cook the remaining lavash in the same way.

**15** Serve immediately.

**16** If the lavash are not to be used at once then, when completely cold, fold and wrap in a tea-towel and then in plastic or wrap and freeze.

**17** When ready to serve them, sprinkle them lightly with water, wrap in a tea-towel and leave for 10 minutes to absorb the moisture and to soften.

## CHAPATI

Thin, round, unleavened bread often sold in Indian restaurants. Similar to the Arab *shapatieh*, this bread is an ideal accompaniment for most meat dishes, but particularly kebabs and stews. Very simple to prepare, the recipe below is from northern India. The wholemeal flour gives the bread an earthy colour and texture.

MAKES EIGHT CHAPATIS

8 oz (225g) wholemeal flour

½ teaspoon salt
2 oz (50g) butter or vegetable fat
1 tablespoon melted clarified butter

**1** Sift the flour and salt into a large mixing bowl.

**2** Add the butter or fat and rub it into the flour until the mixture resembles fine breadcrumbs.

**3** Make a well in the centre and pour in 3 fl oz (90ml) water.

**4** Draw the flour into the water with your fingers and mix well, gradually adding another 2 fl oz (60ml) water.

**5** Form the dough into a ball and place it on a floured working surface.

**6** Knead for about 10 minutes or until it has become smooth and elastic.

**7** Put the dough into a bowl, cover with a cloth and leave to stand for 30 minutes at room temperature.

**8** Divide the dough into eight portions and roll into balls between the palms of your hands.

**9** On a floured surface roll out each ball of dough into a thin round about 6 ins (15cm) across.

**10** Meanwhile heat a heavy-based frying pan or griddle and when it is hot place a circle of dough in it.

**11** When small blisters appear on the surface press the chapati to flatten it.

**12** When the underside is pale golden turn it over and cook the remaining side in the same way.

**13** Remove from the pan and brush on both sides with a little of the clarified butter.

**14** Place on a plate and cover with another plate to keep it warm while you cook the remaining chapatis in the same way.

**15** Serve warm.

## NAAN

*Punjabi flat, leavened bread*

Traditionally this bread is cooked in a *tandoor* – a large clay oven – and it gets its tear-drop shape from being stuck to the wall of the oven and stretching while it cooks. Use it with all the dishes from the Indian subcontinent mentioned in this book as well as with other kebabs.

*1 teaspoon dried yeast*
*¼ pint (150ml) yoghurt*
*3 teaspoons sugar*
*1 egg, beaten*
*2 oz (50g) ghee or butter, melted*
*2 teaspoons salt*

*12 oz (350g) plain flour*
*a little melted ghee or butter for*
  *glazing*
*2 tablespoons poppy seeds or sesame*
  *seeds*

**1** Put the yeast into a small bowl with a little lukewarm water and stir until dissolved.

**2** Leave in a warm place.

**3** Put the yoghurt into a bowl and beat until smooth.

**4** Add ¼ pint (150ml) lukewarm water, sugar, egg, melted ghee and salt, and mix well.

**5** When the yeast has begun to work and there is a froth on the surface, pour the yeast mixture into the bowl with the other liquid ingredients and stir in.

**6** Sift 8 oz (250g) of the flour into a large mixing bowl, make a well in the centre and pour in the liquid mixture.

**7** Stir and knead until you have a smooth batter.

**8** Now slowly knead in the remaining flour until you have a soft dough.

**9** Remove to a lightly floured surface and knead for 10 to 15 minutes until it is smooth and elastic. Dust with flour if it is a little sticky.

**10** Form the dough into a ball, put into a large bowl, cover with a damp cloth and set aside in a warm place for 2 to 3 hours.

**11** Remove the dough from the bowl and knead for a few minutes to remove the air bubbles and to ensure a good rise and even texture.

**12** Preheat oven to 450°F (230°C, gas 8) and oil two large baking sheets.

**13** Divide the dough into six to eight balls, depending on the size of bread wanted, and leave to rest for 10 minutes.

**14** Pat the balls into circles making them slightly thinner in the centre and thicker around the rim.

**15** Now pull one end outwards – like a large tear-drop.

**16** Brush both sides with ghee and place two loaves on each oiled baking sheet.

**17** Sprinkle the tops with the poppy seeds or sesame seeds.

**18** Bake in the oven for about 10 minutes or until nicely puffed and golden brown.

**19** Repeat with the remaining loaves.

**20** Serve immediately in order to appreciate the fragrance.

## KELA PACH CHADI
### *Bananas in spiced yoghurt*

From Hyderabad, India; usually served as an accompaniment to a curry meal, but also very good with kebabs.

*3 large ripe bananas*
*3 tablespoons freshly grated or*
  *desiccated coconut*
*½ pint (300ml) yoghurt*
*2 tablespoons lemon juice*
*2 teaspoons sugar*

*½ teaspoon salt*
*⅛ teaspoon chilli powder, optional*
*1 teaspoon ghee or oil*
*1 teaspoon cumin seeds*
*½ teaspoon black mustard seeds*

**1** Peel and slice bananas. There should be approximately two cups of sliced banana.

**2** If using desiccated coconut, sprinkle 1 tablespoon hot water over it and mix until coconut is evenly moistened.

**3** Season the yoghurt with lemon juice, sugar, salt and chilli powder, and stir in the bananas and coconut.

**4** In a small saucepan heat the ghee and fry the cumin and mustard seeds until the mustard seeds pop.

**5** Pour this over the yoghurt mixture and fold in.

**6** Serve.

# SAUCES, DRESSINGS AND DRINKS

### ORGA'S YOGHURT DRESSING

This recipe is Irfan Orga's, from his book *Cooking with Yogurt*. An extremely versatile dressing, which goes well with poultry and fish as well as salads.

1½ tablespoons sifted flour
½ teaspoon sugar
½ teaspoon salt
½ teaspoon dry mustard
2 fl oz (60ml) tarragon vinegar

2 egg yolks
¼ pint (150ml) olive oil
2½ fl oz (75ml) yoghurt
2 tablespoons minced chives

1 Into a saucepan put the flour, sugar, salt, dry mustard and vinegar, and 6 fl oz (200ml) water.
2 Cook over a low heat until the sauce thickens, stirring all the time. Bring to the boil for a minute or so and remove from the heat.
3 Beat in the egg yolks and continue beating.
4 Add the olive oil gradually.
5 Chill well, for at least 4 hours.
6 An hour before serving add the yoghurt and chives. Beat for 1 minute.

### HORSERADISH SAUCE

An adaptation of the classic French version. Goes well with cold cuts, roasts and kebabs.

1 tablespoon butter
1 tablespoon sifted flour
1 oz (25g) grated horseradish
½ pint (300ml) yoghurt

2 tablespoons tarragon vinegar
½ teaspoon caster sugar
1 teaspoon salt
½ teaspoon cayenne pepper

166

1  Melt the butter in a pan, add flour and stir until smooth.
2  Add the horseradish and yoghurt, stirring all the time.
3  Bring to the boil, lower the heat and cook until thick and creamy.
4  Add the vinegar, sugar, salt and cayenne and stir well.
5  Remove from heat and allow to cool. Refrigerate for 1 to 2 hours.
6  Serve cold.


## TARÇINLI YOGURT SOS
### *Cinnamon yoghurt sauce*

An Anatolian favourite.

*½ pint (300ml) yoghurt*
*2 teaspoons sugar*
*1 teaspoon ground cinnamon*

1  Pour the yoghurt into a serving bowl, add the sugar and mix well.
2  Sprinkle with cinnamon.
3  Serve as an accompaniment to meat dishes, grills, roasts, etc.


## SUGHTOROV MADZOON
### *Garlic yoghurt sauce*

Yoghurt and garlic go very well together and this recipe is by far the most popular throughout the Middle East. It can be served with virtually any dish, hot or cold.

*½ pint (300ml) yoghurt*
*1 clove garlic, crushed*
*¼ teaspoon salt*
*½ teaspoon dried mint*
*1 spring onion, finely chopped (optional)*

1  Pour the yoghurt into a bowl.
2  Mix the garlic and salt together, add to the yoghurt and mix well.
3  Sprinkle the top with dried mint and the onion if using it.
4  Serve with fried vegetables, lamb or beef dishes, etc.

## YOGHURT SALAD DRESSING

Yoghurt enlivens the flavour of this creamy salad dressing, which is particularly good with coleslaw, but can accompany any green salad.

MAYONNAISE

2 egg yolks, at room
   temperature
½ teaspoon salt
⅛ teaspoon white pepper
¾ teaspoon dry mustard
8 fl oz (250ml) olive oil, at room
   temperature

1 tablespoon white wine,
   vinegar or lemon juice

4 tablespoons yoghurt
1 teaspoon sugar
½ teaspoon salt
1 tablespoon grated onion
1 tablespoon finely chopped
   celery

**1** To prepare the mayonnaise, place the egg yolks, salt, pepper and mustard in a mixing bowl.

**2** Using a wire whisk, beat until thoroughly blended.

**3** Add the oil, a few drops at a time, whisking constantly.

**4** Do not add the oil too quickly or the mayonnaise will curdle.

**5** After the mayonnaise has thickened the oil may be added a little more rapidly.

**6** Beat in a few drops of vinegar or lemon juice from time to time to prevent the mayonnaise becoming too thick.

**7** When all the oil has been added, stir in the remaining vinegar or lemon juice.

**8** Blend the mayonnaise with the yoghurt, mixing well with a wooden spoon.

**9** Add the remaining ingredients and beat for 1 minute.

**10** Use immediately.

## YOGHURT MAYONNAISE

Excellent for chicken or poached fish, boiled eggs and salads.

¼ pint (150ml) yoghurt
¼ pint (150ml) mayonnaise
1 teaspoon Dijon mustard
1 tablespoon lemon juice

2 tablespoons chopped parsley
2 tablespoons chopped chives
2 tablespoons fresh tarragon,
   chopped

1 In a bowl whisk the yoghurt and mayonnaise until well blended.
2 Add the mustard, lemon juice and the herbs.
3 Mix well.
4 Serve.

## AVOCADO YOGHURT SAUCE

Serve as a sauce for shrimp or seafood cocktails. This recipe is from Israel.

*1 medium-size avocado*
*1 tablespoon fresh lemon juice*
*2 fl oz (60ml) bottled chilli sauce*

*1 teaspoon Worcestershire sauce*
*4 fl oz (120ml) yoghurt*
*salt and pepper to taste*

1 Peel the avocado and cut in half.
2 Remove stone and mash the flesh to a purée.
3 Add the lemon juice and mix well.
4 Add all the remaining ingredients and chill.

## WATERCRESS YOGHURT DRESSING

A very tasty dressing for a seafood dish or a shrimp cocktail.

*4 fl oz (120ml) mayonnaise*
*2 fl oz (60ml) tomato purée*
*2 teaspoons fresh lemon juice*
*2 teaspoons prepared horseradish
    sauce*

*salt and pepper to taste*
*8 fl oz (250ml) yoghurt*
*1 large bunch watercress, washed
    and finely chopped*

1 Mix all the ingredients, except the watercress, together and place in the refrigerator to chill.
2 Stir in the watercress just before serving.

## MADZNOV GANACHI SALSA
*Yoghurt herb dressing*

Serve with fish dishes.

*½ pint (300 ml) yoghurt*
*2 tablespoons finely chopped celery*
  *leaves*
*1 teaspoon chopped parsley*
*1 tablespoon chopped chives*
*1 tablespoon grated horseradish*

*1 tablespoon lemon juice*
*½ teaspoon paprika*
*½ teaspoon salt*
*1 clove garlic, crushed*
*1 teaspoon* sumak *powder*
  *(see p. 198)*

**1** Beat the yoghurt until creamy.
**2** Stir in all remaining ingredients, except the *sumak*.
**3** Taste and adjust seasoning if necessary.
**4** Sprinkle *sumak* over.

## YOGHURT FISH SAUCE

A piquant sauce that goes well with hot or cold cooked fish.

*¼ pint (150ml) yoghurt*
*¼ pint (150ml) mayonnaise*
*1 teaspoon lemon juice*
*½ teaspoon cayenne pepper*
*1 tablespoon chopped parsley*

**1** In a bowl mix the yoghurt and mayonnaise, and then add the lemon juice and cayenne pepper. Stir well.
**2** Sprinkle chopped parsley on top and serve.

## YOGHURT TARTARE SAUCE

Serve this sauce with fish.

*¼ pint (150ml) mayonnaise*
*¼ pint (150ml) yoghurt*
*2 tablespoons finely chopped green*
  *pepper*
*1 tablespoon finely chopped onion*

*2 tablespoons finely chopped sweet*
  *pickle*
*1 tablespoon finely chopped parsley*
*1 tablespoon capers*
*salt and pepper to taste*

Mix all the ingredients together and chill.

## SAUCE HOLLANDAISE WITH YOGHURT

An alternative to the well-known hollandaise. Serve hot or cold with fish or other lightly flavoured dishes and with grilled or fried vegetables.

*4 egg yolks, beaten*
*8 fl oz (250ml) yoghurt stabilized*
  *with 1 egg or 1 tablespoon plain*
  *flour*
*3 oz (75g) butter*

*salt and pepper to taste*
*1 teaspoon grated lemon rind or 2*
  *teaspoons tarragon vinegar*
*1 teaspoon lemon juice*

**1** Strain the beaten egg yolks into the top of a double saucepan over boiling water.

**2** Add the yoghurt slowly and stir constantly until the mixture thickens.

**3** Whisk the butter, 1 oz (25g) at a time, into the sauce, until it is smooth and glossy.

**4** Add salt and pepper to taste and the lemon rind or tarragon vinegar, and lemon juice.

**5** Remove from the heat immediately.

## YOGHURT MUSTARD SAUCE

I find this sauce excellent with fish and chicken dishes, but especially with cooked vegetables such as celery, leeks and broccoli. The *sumak* powder gives the sauce colour as well as flavour.

*¼ pint (150ml) yoghurt*
*2 egg yolks*
*1 teaspoon lemon juice*
*½ teaspoon salt*
*¼ teaspoon black pepper*

*½ teaspoon fennel seeds*
*1 teaspoon sumak powder*
  *(see p. 198)*
*1 teaspoon Dijon mustard*

**1** In a bowl beat the egg yolks, yoghurt and lemon juice thoroughly.

**2** Place the bowl over a pan of simmering water. Cook the sauce by this method for 12 to 15 minutes, stirring frequently until the sauce is thick.

**3** Add all the spices and seasonings.

**4** Stir well and pour into a sauce-boat.

## TKEMALI SAUCE
*Prune yoghurt sauce*

This is a popular sauce from the Caucasus and is traditionally eaten with lamb or pork kebabs and *dapakhav madznou* (see p. 133).

*½ lb (250g) prunes*
*2 cloves garlic, crushed*
*¼ teaspoon salt*
*2 tablespoons finely chopped fresh coriander*

*¼ teaspoon black pepper*
*1 tablespoon lemon juice*
*pinch of cayenne pepper*
*3 tablespoons yoghurt*

**1** Wash the prunes and place in a saucepan with enough water to cover.

**2** Bring to the boil and simmer for 10 to 15 minutes.

**3** Strain the prunes into a sieve and reserve the liquid.

**4** Leave the prunes until cool enough to handle and then remove and discard the stones.

**5** Rub the prunes through a sieve and then dilute with some of the reserved liquid until the sauce has the consistency of thick cream.

**6** Stir in the garlic, salt, black pepper and coriander.

**7** Return the sauce to the pan and bring to the boil.

**8** Stir in the lemon juice and cayenne pepper and remove from the heat.

**9** Serve at room temperature; spoon the yoghurt over the top and swirl into the sauce.

## YOGURTLI TOREOTU SOS
*Dill yoghurt sauce*

A recipe from Ismir in Turkey.
Serve with cooked meat, poultry or fish.

*1 oz (25g) butter*
*1 onion, finely chopped*
*2 tablespoons flour*
*salt and pepper to taste*

*¾ pint (450ml) hot chicken stock*
*juice of ½ lemon*
*¼ pint (150ml) yoghurt*
*2 tablespoons chopped fresh dill*

**1** Melt the butter in a saucepan and sauté the onion until it is soft and translucent.

**2** Stir in the flour and cook for 1 minute, stirring constantly.

**3** Season with salt and pepper.

**4** Gradually add the hot stock and cook slowly, stirring constantly until it thickens.

**5** Stir in the lemon juice, yoghurt and dill and heat through, but do not boil.

**6** Remove from the heat immediately.

## YOGHURT CHEESE SAUCE

Try making cheese sauce with yoghurt instead of milk. It is good with cooked eggs, vegetables, pasta, etc.

*2 oz (50g) butter*
*3 tablespoons flour*
*¾ pint (450ml) yoghurt*
*½ teaspoon paprika*

*4 oz (100g) grated cheese (Gouda,*
   *Edam, Cheddar, etc.)*
*½ teaspoon salt*
*dash of black pepper*

**1** Melt the butter in a saucepan.

**2** Remove from the heat and stir in the flour.

**3** Cook for 1 to 1½ minutes.

**4** Beat the yoghurt vigorously and gradually add to the pan.

**5** Cook slowly and stir continuously until the sauce thickens.

**6** Mix in the cheese, paprika, salt and pepper.

**7** Cook slowly until the cheese melts.

**8** Serve as a topping with fish or pancakes.

## MADZNOV-BANRI SALTSA
*Cheese sauce*

A family recipe. Serve with cooked eggs, pasta or vegetables.

*1½ oz (40g) butter*
*3 tablespoons flour*
*6 fl oz (200ml) hot milk*
*6 fl oz (200ml) yoghurt*
*1 teaspoon prepared strong mustard*

*4 oz (125g) grated Gouda or Edam*
   *cheese*
*¼ teaspoon paprika*
*salt and pepper to taste*

173

**1** Melt butter in a saucepan and stir in the flour.
**2** Cook for 1 minute.
**3** Gradually add the milk and then the yoghurt and cook slowly, stirring constantly, until thickened and smooth.
**4** Mix in the cheese, mustard, paprika, salt and pepper and cook slowly, stirring until the cheese melts.

## YOGHURT MILK SHAKE

You can make milk shakes with yoghurt, using any kind of milk shake syrup, e.g. chocolate, pineapple, banana, vanilla. It makes an excellent drink.

SERVES TWO

> *4 tablespoons of the syrup of your choice*
> *1 scoop of ice cream of the same flavour*
> *½ pint (300ml) milk*
> *¼ pint (150ml) natural yoghurt*

**1** Put the ingredients in a blender and mix thoroughly.
**2** Pour into two glasses.

## TAN

This is a refreshing yoghurt drink, popular throughout the Middle East. It is known as *Ayran* in Arabic-speaking lands, *dough* in Iran and *tan* among Armenian-speaking people. It is ideal accompaniment for kebabs and perfect as a summer drink. The proportions given here are for one person. They can be increased in proportion to the number required.

SERVES ONE

*2 tablespoons yoghurt*
*½ pint (300ml) water*
*¼ teaspoon salt*
*¼ teaspoon dried mint*
*some ice cubes*

1 Spoon the yoghurt into a glass and very gradually stir in the water to make a smooth mixture.

2 Stir in the salt and mint.

3 Drop in a few ice cubes and serve.

### Tan with soda water

In Iran, soda water is often used instead of plain water. It has a delightful flavour and the same quantities are used.

### LUSSI

This Indian version of *tan* or *dough* is the most popular drink on the Indian subcontinent. It is drunk in two ways, either sweet (*meeta*) or salted (*numkeen*). It is a perfect accompaniment for kebabs at a summer party.

SERVES SIX
¾ *pint (450ml) yoghurt*
¾ *pint (450ml) milk*
*juice of one lemon*

½ *teaspoon* kewra *extract*
*(see p. 198) – rosewater*
*can be substituted*
either *sugar* or *salt to taste*

1 In a large jug or mixing bowl put the yoghurt, milk, lemon juice and *kewra* extract or rosewater.

2 Stir well until the mixture is smooth.

3 Add the sugar or salt to taste and stir.

4 Pour into individual glasses and serve with some ice cubes and slices of lemon.

# SWEETS AND CAKES

### ANOUSH-MADZOONI KREMA
*Sweet yoghurt dressing*

This recipe from the 'old country' is usually added to fresh fruit salads or any fruit dessert. It is excellent with strawberries and makes an interesting change from cream.

½ pint (300ml) yoghurt
2 tablespoons honey (or 4
   tablespoons caster sugar)
1 tablespoon orange juice (or grape
   or pineapple juice)

½ teaspoon lemon juice
1 teaspoon grated lemon rind
pinch of salt
a few drops of rosewater

1 In a bowl, beat the yoghurt until frothy.
2 Add the other ingredients.
3 Mix well.
4 Serve with fresh fruit salad, strawberries or as a topping to any other fruit.

### APPLE YOGHURT FOOL

An interesting new use of yoghurt in an apple fool. Instead of cherries you can use any other glacé fruit and angelica leaves for decoration.

1 lb (½kg) cooking apples
1 lemon rind
3 cloves
about 1 tablespoon brown sugar –
   the exact amount will depend on

the apples and on individual taste
2 eggs, separated
¼ pint (150ml) yoghurt
5–6 glacé cherries, halved

1 Peel, core and slice the apples.

2 Place in a saucepan, and add the lemon rind, cloves and 2 tablespoons water.

3 Cover and simmer over a low heat until the apples are soft.

4 Discard the lemon rind and cloves.

5 Put the apples and sugar in a liquidizer and blend.

6 Return the purée to the saucepan.

7 Add the egg yolks to the apple purée and stir continuously on a low heat for 5 to 8 minutes, or until the egg yolks have thickened the purée.

8 Remove the pan from the heat, stir in the yoghurt until thoroughly blended and leave to cool.

9 Whisk the egg whites until stiff and fold into the cool apple purée.

10 Divide into individual dishes or pile into a serving dish and decorate with cherries.


### APPLES WITH PORT

A lovely dessert which is simple and cheap to make. Use home-made yoghurt to get the required consistency and that special flavour of home cooking.

*1 lb (½kg) cooking apples*
*2 oz (50g) butter*
*4 oz (100g) brown sugar*
*1 teaspoon cinnamon*
*a few drops of rosewater*

*2½ fl oz (75ml) port*
*¼ pint (150ml) yoghurt*
*1 tablespoon pistachio nuts, finely*
  *chopped*

1 Peel the apples and slice thickly.

2 Melt the butter in a saucepan, add the apple slices and cook, turning constantly, until soft and brown.

3 Add the sugar, cinnamon, rosewater and port and cook for a further 4 to 5 minutes. Taste and adjust if necessary.

4 Lift out apples with a slotted spoon and place in serving glasses.

5 Strain the sauce and pour into each dish.

6 Spoon the yoghurt over the apples, sprinkle with the pistachios and serve.

## APRICOT AND YOGHURT CUSTARD

A tasty, attractive sweet; simple to prepare.

*4 oz (100g) dried apricots, soaked overnight in cold water*
*½ pint (300ml) yoghurt*
*2 egg yolks*
*1 tablespoon brown sugar*
*2 tablespoons chopped pistachio nuts*

**1** Cut the apricots into small pieces and put into a 1½ pint (1l) dish.
**2** Beat the yoghurt and egg yolks together and pour over the apricots.
**3** Place the dish in a baking tin and pour enough cold water into the tin to come half-way up the dish.
**4** Place in an oven preheated to 325°F (160°C, gas 3) and bake for 30 to 40 minutes until just set.
**5** Mix the brown sugar and pistachio nuts together and sprinkle over the top.
**6** Serve cold.

## APRICOT AND YOGHURT MOUSSE

A delicious sweet with a slightly tart flavour, often welcome after a spicy or heavy main course. This recipe adapts easily to other fruits, e.g. raspberries, pears, strawberries, blackcurrants, etc.

*1 tablespoon gelatine*
*3 tablespoons orange juice*
*1 large tin (14–15 oz, 400–450g) apricot halves*
*1 tablespoon sugar (optional)*
*½ pint (300ml) yoghurt*

*2½ fl oz (75ml) double cream, whipped until stiff*
*1 oz (25g) pistachio nuts, crushed or ground until they are like fine breadcrumbs*

**1** Put the gelatine and orange juice in a small bowl and place over a saucepan of simmering water.
**2** Stir until the gelatine dissolves and the mixture becomes clear.
**3** Drain the fruit; place it in a liquidizer with just sufficient orange juice to make a thick purée and blend.
**4** Empty the purée into a large bowl.

5 Stir in the gelatine mixture, sugar, yoghurt and whipped cream.

6 Turn the mixture into a wetted 2 pint (1l) mould or serving dish and chill until firm.

7 If using a mould then turn the mousse out and sprinkle with the nuts.

8 Otherwise simply sprinkle the nuts over the mousse in the dish.

9 Serve immediately.

## ARMENIACA
### *Apricots with yoghurt*

This recipe was given to me by the chef of the Geghart restaurant in Armenia. It was created in honour of both the country and its fruit, the apricot (*Prunus armeniaca*). The recipe makes clever use of apricots.

*1 lb (½kg) apricots, stoned and
    halved*
*¼ pint (150ml) apricot brandy*
*8 oz (250g) caster sugar*
*2 oz (50g) butter*

*4 eggs, separated*
*¼ pint (150ml) yoghurt*
*2½ fl oz (75ml) double cream*
*2 tablespoons pistachio nuts,
    crushed*

1 Pour 1 pint (600ml) water into a large saucepan, add the apricots and apricot brandy and cook over a moderate heat until the apricots are nearly tender.

2 Remove the fruit with a large spoon and set aside.

3 Add the sugar to the pan and raise the heat. Boil for 10 minutes until the water is reduced and the syrup has thickened.

4 Arrange the apricots in an ovenproof dish, dot with butter and bake for 10 to 12 minutes at a medium heat (350°F, 180°C, gas 4).

5 Remove the dish from the oven, add the syrup from the saucepan, return to the oven and cook for a further 15 minutes.

6 Remove the dish from the oven and allow to cool for 5 to 10 minutes.

7 Meanwhile beat the egg yolks until fluid and add to the apricots.

8 Beat the egg whites until stiff and fold into the apricots; return the dish to the oven and bake for a further 12 to 15 minutes.

9 Remove and bring to the table.

**10** In a small bowl beat the yoghurt, cream and pistachio nuts together.

**11** Pour over the apricot dish and serve immediately.

### MOZ-BI-LABAN
*Banana yoghurt*

A charmingly simple dessert from the Mediterranean coast where very sweet bananas are grown. A childhood favourite.

> *1 pint (600ml) yoghurt*
> *4 ripe bananas*
> *sugar to taste*
> *1 teaspoon cinnamon*

**1** Pour the yoghurt into a bowl and beat until creamy.

**2** Slice the bananas thinly and stir very gently into the yoghurt.

**3** Stir in a little sugar at a time until it suits your taste.

**4** Spoon into a large serving dish or into individual dishes, sprinkle with the cinnamon and serve.

### TOUZ MADZNOV
*Figs in yoghurt*

A Middle Eastern delicacy which my friends and I used to love when we were young. We were able to pick the figs off the tree in our garden. It is extremely easy to make, but the fresh figs give it an exotic air. *Ser* or *kaymak* is the thick Middle Eastern cream that is normally cut with a knife. Clotted cream makes an excellent substitute if you can get it.

> *12 fresh figs*
> *¼ pint (150ml)* ser *or clotted or double cream*
> *½ pint (300ml)* anoush-madzooni krema *(see p. 176)*
> *cinnamon*
> *1 tablespoon pistachios*

1 Drop the figs into a bowl of hot water, leave for 2 to 3 minutes and then drain.

2 Peel off the skins and quarter the figs.

3 Whisk the cream a little and add to the yoghurt sauce.

4 Spoon a little of the yoghurt sauce into four to six serving glasses.

5 Divide the figs between the glasses and then spoon the remaining yoghurt over the top.

6 Sprinkle with cinnamon and pistachios. Chill for at least an hour before serving.

## MAST BA HOOLU
### *Peaches with yoghurt*

This is a simple sweet from Tehran, Iran, which is equally delicious hot or cold.

> *4 large, ripe peaches*
> *2 tablespoons brown sugar*
> *½ teaspoon ground cinnamon*
> *½ pint (300ml) stabilized yoghurt*
> *4 tablespoons caster sugar*

1 Drop the peaches into boiling water for 10 seconds and then plunge them immediately into cold water.

2 Skin them, cut in half to remove the stones and then slice.

3 Arrange the slices in four individual soufflé dishes.

4 In a small dish mix the brown sugar and cinnamon and sprinkle over the peaches.

5 Spoon the yoghurt over the peaches.

6 Sprinkle each dish with 1 tablespoon of the caster sugar.

7 Heat the grill until it is red hot.

8 Place the dishes under the grill and leave until the sugar melts and caramelizes.

9 Serve hot or cold.

## FUSTUKHE-WAH-ANNANAS
*Pineapple with yoghurt and pistachio nuts*

This is an unusual, highly successful combination, from Lebanon.

SERVES SIX

3 tablespoons self-raising flour
4 tablespoons caster sugar
1 teaspoon bicarbonate of soda
pinch of salt

4 eggs, separated
¼ pineapple, pulped and drained
½ pint (300ml) yoghurt
12 pineapple cubes, fresh or tinned
4 tablespoons chopped pistachio nuts

1  Mix the flour, sugar, soda and salt together in a bowl.
2  Place the egg yolks in a small bowl and beat until they are lemon yellow.
3  Add to the dry ingredients together with the pulped pineapple and stir well.
4  Whisk the yoghurt, add to the mixture and stir until well blended.
5  Whisk the egg whites until stiff and then fold gently into the mixture.
6  Pour the mixture into six individual ovenproof dishes.
7  Set the dishes in a shallow pan and pour sufficient cold water into the pan to come half-way up the dishes.
8  Place in an oven preheated to 350°F (180°C, gas 4) and cook for 45 to 60 minutes, or until the contents of the dishes are firm.
9  Meanwhile roll the pineapple cubes in the chopped nuts.
10  Garnish each dish with two of the cubes and serve.

## NOORANOUSH
*Pomegranates and yoghurt*

An Armenian recipe; extremely attractive both in texture and colour. It makes an excellent dessert.

6 oz (175g) caster sugar
1 teaspoon lemon juice
4 tablespoons rosewater
2 large pomegranates
2 medium pomegranates

2 tablespoons coarse dry
    breadcrumbs – you could use
    crushed digestive biscuits
    instead
4 fl oz (120ml) yoghurt

2 tablespoons double cream or,
  preferably, clotted cream

2 tablespoons pistachio nuts,
  chopped

**1** First make the syrup by placing in a small saucepan the sugar and lemon juice and ½ pint (300ml) water.

**2** Bring to the boil and then simmer for 10 to 15 minutes, or until the syrup forms a film over the back of a spoon.

**3** Stir in the rosewater and set aside.

**4** Meanwhile cut all the pomegranates in half and remove the seeds.

**5** Retain the large pomegranate halves and remove any pith remaining in them.

**6** Put the seeds and breadcrumbs or crushed biscuits in a bowl, mix and then mash.

**7** Spoon the mixture into the pomegranate shells and pack tightly.

**8** Pour the syrup slowly over the mixture, giving it time to soak through.

**9** Place in the refrigerator and chill for 2 to 4 hours.

**10** Whisk the yoghurt and cream together and spoon over the pomegranates.

**11** Sprinkle the chopped nuts over the top and serve immediately.


## FRUIT AND NUT YOGHURT PUDDING

A new and exciting recipe I found in a health magazine. I like it very much.

grated rind and juice of 1 orange
½ oz (15g) gelatine
1 pint (600ml) yoghurt
1 oz (25g) brown sugar
1 oz (25g) stoned dates, chopped

1 oz (25g) walnuts or hazelnuts,
  finely chopped
1 oz (25g) dried raisins
a few stewed apricots for garnish

**1** Having grated the rind, slice the orange in half and squeeze out the juice.

**2** Pour the juice into a small saucepan and sprinkle in the gelatine.

**3** Place over a low heat and allow to melt slowly and swell.

**4** Pour the yoghurt into a bowl, add the melted gelatine and sugar, beat well to mix and leave to cool.

**5** When on the verge of setting stir in the fruit and nuts.

**6** Rub the inside of a 1¼–1½ pint (¾–1l) jelly mould with a few drops of oil.

**7** Pour in the pudding and place in the refrigerator to set.

**8** Turn the pudding on to a serving dish and garnish with a few stewed apricots.

## YAOURTI ME MELI
### *Yoghurt with honey*

This is an unusual alternative to cream and is a beautiful accompaniment to desserts and cakes. Try it for breakfast. It is very popular throughout Greece.

*¼ pint (150ml) clear honey*
*1 teaspoon grated lemon rind*
*1 teaspoon grated orange rind*
*1 teaspoon white wine*

*1 teaspoon orange juice*
*½ teaspoon lemon juice*
*1¼ pints (¾l) yoghurt*

**1** Pour the honey into a mixing bowl and add the lemon and orange rind and the wine.

**2** Beat until smooth.

**3** Add the orange and lemon juice and whisk until frothy.

**4** Add the yoghurt and stir well.

**5** Place in the refrigerator to chill.

## CHOCOLATE AND NUT CREAM

A delicious dessert with that tang which only yoghurt can give.

*1 pint (600ml) yoghurt*
*5 tablespoons chocolate sauce*
*4 oz (100g) mixed nuts, roughly chopped, e.g. walnuts, hazelnuts,*

*almonds and pistachio nuts – if you can afford them*
*4 oz (100g) small macaroons or ratafia biscuits*

**1** Pour the yoghurt into a bowl, add the chocolate sauce and stir well until you have a rippled effect.

**2** Divide half the nuts and biscuits between four glasses or sorbet dishes.

**3** Spoon some of the yoghurt mixture over the top.

**4** Add the remaining biscuits.

**5** Spoon in the remaining yoghurt mixture.

**6** Top with the remaining nuts.

**7** Chill in the refrigerator and then serve.

## RAS GULA
### *Panir balls in syrup*

A great Indian sweet. If made well these walnut-shaped balls of cream cheese, simmered in a syrup flavoured with cardamon, are mouthwatering.

panir–*made from 3 pints (1¾l) milk and 3 tablespoons lemon juice (see p. 19)*
*3 teaspoons very fine semolina*

*about 12 sugar cubes*
*1 lb (500g) sugar*
*6–8 cardamon pods, bruised*
*2–3 tablespoons rosewater*

**1** Empty the *panir* on to a working top and knead with the heel of your hand for 2 to 3 minutes.

**2** Add the semolina and knead for a further 3 minutes until the cheese is smooth. When the palm of your hand becomes greasy it is ready for moulding.

**3** Divide the mixture into about twelve walnut-sized balls.

**4** Mould each one around a cube of sugar and roll into a ball between your palms.

**5** Place the sugar and 1½ pints (1l) water in a large saucepan and bring slowly to the boil, stirring constantly until the sugar dissolves.

**6** Simmer for 5 minutes.

**7** Pour a quarter of the syrup into a jug and set aside.

**8** Add the cardamon pods and the cheese balls to the syrup remaining in the saucepan and bring to the boil.

**9** Lower the heat and simmer until the balls swell and become spongy. This will take about 1 hour.

**10** When the syrup thickens add a little of the reserved syrup. Stir well.

**11** Remove from the heat and stir in the rosewater.

**12** Serve warm. They are very rich – serve only one or two per person to start with, spooning a little of the syrup over them.

## HONEY AND GINGER CHEESECAKE

Simple, tasty cheesecake made of ginger biscuits, honey and yoghurt. Ideal tea-time accompaniment.

BASE
*8 oz (250g) ginger biscuits*
*4 oz (125g) butter, melted*

FILLING
*8 oz (250g) cream cheese*
*¼ pint (150ml) yoghurt*

*2 tablespoons honey*
*½ level tablespoon gelatine*

DECORATION
*2½ fl oz (75ml) double cream,*
  *whipped*
*pieces of crystallized ginger*

**1** Crush biscuits in a polythene bag with a rolling pin or in a blender.

**2** Mix with the butter and press evenly over the base of a loose-bottomed 8 in (20cm) cake tin.

**3** Put the cream cheese, yoghurt and honey into a bowl and mix until smooth.

**4** Place the gelatine with 2 tablespoons water in a small bowl over a saucepan of hot water and stir until the gelatine has dissolved and the mixture is clear.

**5** Stir this into the cheese mixture.

**6** Pour into the cake tin and leave to set.

**7** Decorate with pieces of crystallized ginger and piped whipped cream.

## SMETANIK CHEESECAKE
*Russian raspberry cheesecake with yoghurt*

This is a traditional Russian recipe, normally made with soured cream. I have tried it with yoghurt instead and the result was beautiful. You can vary the fruit and use bilberries, blackberries or even gooseberries instead. As it is not possible to obtain fresh fruit all the year round use tinned or bottled fruit instead – you will find the results equally acceptable.

1 lb (500g) digestive biscuits,
    crushed
4 oz (125g) butter, melted
½ teaspoon cinnamon
10 oz (300g) cream cheese
1 egg
½ pint (300ml) yoghurt
2 oz (50g) caster sugar
3 teaspoons lemon juice
¼ teaspoon salt

TOPPING
1 lb (½kg) fresh raspberries or
    15–16 oz (450–500g) tin
    raspberries
sugar to taste if using fresh fruit
1 tablespoon cornflour
1 tablespoon lemon juice
¼ teaspoon cinnamon

1 Mix the crushed biscuits with the melted butter and the cinnamon and press evenly over the base of a loose-bottomed 9 in (23cm) round cake tin.

2 Place the cream cheese, egg, yoghurt, caster sugar, lemon juice and salt in a large mixing bowl.

3 Beat the ingredients together until smooth – use an electric mixer if you have one.

4 Spoon the mixture over the biscuit base.

5 Place in an oven preheated to 375°F (190°C, gas 5) and bake for 40 to 45 minutes.

6 Remove from the oven and leave to cool.

7 Meanwhile make the topping:
   (a) If using fresh raspberries, stew with about 2½ fl oz (75ml) water until just soft, but not reduced to a pulp. The fruit should be as intact as possible. Sweeten with sugar.
   (b) If using tinned raspberries, strain and reserve the syrup.

8 In a small saucepan blend the cornflour with a few tablespoons of the cool fruit syrup and then stir in the remaining syrup.

9 Bring to the boil stirring constantly and cook for about 3 minutes.

10 Remove from the heat and leave to cool.

11 Stir in the raspberries, lemon juice and cinnamon.

12 Pour this raspberry topping over the cheesecake and chill for a few hours in the refrigerator.

## AWAMAAT
### *Arab doughnuts*

Doughnuts have been traditional fare in the Middle East for longer than in Europe. There are many variations. This recipe is from Syria. It does not use yeast or baking powder.

SYRUP
*1½ lb (750g) sugar*
*2 teaspoons lemon juice*
*2 teaspoons rosewater essence*

DOUGH
*1 lb (500g) self-raising flour*
*1 teaspoon bicarbonate of soda*
*16 fl oz (½l) yoghurt*

*1¼ pints (¾l) vegetable oil*
*2 oz (50g) finely chopped walnuts*
  *and pistachios for garnish*

 **1** First prepare the syrup by putting the sugar and lemon juice in a small pan with 1 pint (600ml) water and bringing to the boil.
 **2** Simmer until the syrup thickens and coats the back of the spoon.
 **3** Remove from the heat and stir in the rosewater essence. Keep hot.
 **4** Prepare the dough by sifting the flour and bicarbonate of soda into a large mixing bowl.
 **5** Gradually add the yoghurt and knead well until you have a soft smooth dough.
 **6** Put the oil in a large saucepan and heat until hot.
 **7** Break off small pieces of the dough and roll into balls about the size of marbles.
 **8** Drop a few at a time into the hot oil and cook, turning frequently, until they are golden brown all over.
 **9** Remove with a slotted spoon and drop into the hot syrup.
 **10** Stir them around and remove to a large plate.
 **11** Repeat until you have used all the dough.
 **12** Stack the doughnuts on a large serving plate, sprinkle with the nuts and serve.

## JALEBI
*Fried batter sweetmeats*

This Indian sweet, perhaps one of the most eye-catching and popular, is very similar to one I remember tasting in the Middle East called *mushabek*. *Mushabek* is whirled round and round in beautiful circles. Try making the *jalebi* in this way by using an icing bag.

To give a brilliant orange colour to the sweetmeats add 1½ teaspoons of liquid orange colouring or any other colour of your choice.

| | |
|---|---|
| 12 oz (350g) plain flour | SYRUP |
| ½ oz (15g) dried yeast | 1 lb (500g) sugar |
| ¼ pint (150ml) yoghurt | pinch of ground saffron |
| 1½ teaspoons orange food colouring | 4 cloves |
| | 1 tablespoon rosewater |
| | vegetable oil |

**1** Sift flour into a large bowl, add the yeast, yoghurt and sufficient warm water to form a batter.

**2** Beat food colouring of choice into the batter.

**3** Cover and stand in a warm place for 3 to 4 hours.

**4** Meanwhile make the syrup in a small saucepan by dissolving the sugar in 1 pint (600ml) water over a low heat.

**5** Stir in the saffron and cloves.

**6** Bring to the boil and then simmer until the syrup thickens.

**7** Remove from the heat, add the rosewater and set aside.

**8** When the batter is ready, take a deep frying pan or a large saucepan and half fill with vegetable oil. Heat until nearly boiling.

**9** Using either an icing bag or a narrow funnel allow the batter to run into the hot oil to form either the traditional figure-of-eight or double circle whirls.

**10** Fry, turning constantly for about 1 minute until crisp and golden on both sides.

**11** Lift out with a slotted spoon and drop into the syrup.

**12** Let it soak for a few minutes – not more than 5 or it will go soggy – and then lift on to a plate.

**13** When all the *jalebi* are cooked and ready arrange them on a clean plate, dust with icing sugar and serve.

## YOGURTLU BOREGI
*Sweet yoghurt pastry*

There are hundreds of recipes for making *boreg* – savoury or sweet pastries using meat, vegetables, cheese, fruits, nuts, etc. This recipe uses yoghurt and sugar and makes a wonderfully cheap and simple dessert.

*3 egg yolks*
*½ teaspoon salt*
*2 tablespoons caster sugar*
*5 tablespoons yoghurt*
*10 oz (300g) self-raising flour, sifted*
*oil for deep frying*

GARNISH
*caster sugar or 4–5 tablespoons*
*  honey diluted with 1 tablespoon*
*  lemon juice*

**1** Put the egg yolks and salt in a large bowl and beat until a light lemony colour.

**2** Add the sugar and the yoghurt and continue to beat.

**3** Gradually fold in the flour and when the mixture thickens knead to a dough.

**4** Transfer to a lightly floured surface and continue kneading until the dough blisters.

**5** Roll out the pastry as thinly as possible.

**6** Cut into ribbons about 1 in (3cm) wide and then cut into strips 3 ins (8cm) long.

**7** Tie each strip in a knot.

**8** Heat the oil and cook a few pastries at a time until they are puffed up and golden. Turn just once.

**9** Lift out with a slotted spoon and drain on kitchen paper.

**10** Pile on to a serving plate and either sprinkle with caster sugar or dilute the honey with the lemon juice and a little water and dribble over the *boreg*. Serve immediately.

## ALMOND GINGERBREAD

This cake has a fairly close texture and is generally quite moist. It should be baked as soon as the ingredients have been mixed together.

8 oz (250g) plain flour
pinch of salt
2 teaspoons ground ginger
1 teaspoon bicarbonate of soda
2 oz (50g) ground almonds
4 oz (100g) margarine

4 oz (100g) golden syrup
4 oz (100g) soft brown sugar
¼ pint (150ml) yoghurt
1 egg, beaten
2 oz (50g) slivered almonds

**1** Line a 7 in (18cm) square or 6½ in (16cm) round cake tin with greased greaseproof paper or non-stick parchment.

**2** Sift the flour, salt, ginger and bicarbonate of soda together into a bowl. Stir in the ground almonds.

**3** Gently melt the margarine, syrup and sugar in a pan over a low heat.

**4** Make a well in the centre of the dry ingredients and pour in the syrup mixture. Add the yoghurt and egg and beat until smooth.

**5** Pour into the prepared tin. Scatter the almonds on top.

**6** Bake in the centre of a moderate oven (325°F, 160°C, gas 3) for 55 to 65 minutes or until the gingerbread is well risen and springy to touch.

**7** Leave in the tin for 15 minutes, then turn out and cool on a wire rack.

## BANANA GÂTEAU

This is a delightful cake from Lebanon. The taste and aroma will speak for themselves. Eat soon as it will only keep for 2–3 days.

4 oz (100g) butter, softened
4 oz (100g) caster sugar
2 eggs
pinch of salt
5 tablespoons yoghurt
2 tablespoons rosewater

2 bananas, cut into thin slices
8 oz (250g) self-raising flour
½ teaspoon bicarbonate of soda
1 oz (25g) chopped almonds
icing sugar

**1** Cream the butter and sugar together until light and fluffy.

**2** Break the eggs into a small bowl, add the salt and whisk with a fork.

**3** Beat the eggs into the butter-sugar mixture.

**4** Beat in the yoghurt and rosewater.

**5** Add the banana slices and stir in very gently.

**6** Sift the flour and soda into the mixture, add the almonds and stir very gently until well blended.

**7** Grease and flour a 7–7½in (17–18cm) round cake tin and spoon in the mixture.

**8** Leave to rest for 30 minutes.

**9** Preheat oven to 350°F (180°C, gas 4).

**10** Bake the cake for approximately 1 hour or until a knife inserted into the centre comes out clean.

**11** Leave to cool and then sift a little icing sugar over the surface.

## ISTANBUL CHOCOLATE CAKE

This is a very popular cake amongst Turks and Armenians, and is cooked especially on festival days. This is an Armenian version using brandy – the Turks, of course, are not permitted to use alcohol, on religious grounds.

*3 oz (75g) plain chocolate*
*4 eggs, separated*
*¼ teaspoon salt*
*1 oz (25g) butter*
*2 oz (50g) vanilla or caster sugar*
*6 oz (150g) self-raising flour*
*¼ teaspoon bicarbonate of soda*
*2½ fl oz (75ml) yoghurt*
*2 fl oz (60ml) brandy*

ICING
*6 oz (150g) melted plain*
   *unsweetened chocolate*
*12 oz (300g) icing sugar, sifted*
*1 oz (25g) butter*
*1 oz (25g) walnuts, finely chopped*
*brandy – sufficient to give the*
   *mixture a spreading consistency*

*crystallized violets*

**1** Put the chocolate with 1 tablespoon water in a small bowl over a pan of hot water and stir until the chocolate melts. Stir well.

**2** Beat the egg yolks with the salt.

**3** Cream the butter and sugar together.

**4** Beat in the egg yolks and melted chocolate.

**5** Sift the flour and soda together and stir into the creamed mixture.

**6** Stir in the yoghurt and the brandy.

**7** Whisk the egg whites until stiff and fold gently into the cake mixture.

**8** Turn into a greased 7½–8 in (18–20cm) round tin.

**9** Bake in an oven preheated to 350°F (180°C, gas 4) for 45 to 50 minutes.

**10** Turn on to a wire rack and cool.

**11** Mix all the icing ingredients together until you have a spreading consistency.

**12** Cut through the middle of the cake.

**13** Sandwich the two halves together with half the icing.

**14** Spread the remainder over the top and decorate with crystallized violets.

## MADZOONOV MIRTKATAN
### *Yoghurt fruit cake*

An exceedingly rich cake from Leninakan, Armenia, full of the dried fruit of the region.

**FRUIT MIXTURE**
*¼ lb (100g) chopped figs*
*¼ lb (100g) chopped dates*
*10 oz (300g) raisins*
*2 oz (50g) mixed peel*
*2 oz (50g) chopped nuts*
*2 oz (50g) chopped pistachio nuts*
*2 fl oz (60ml) orange juice*
*grated rind of ½ orange*
*2 tablespoons lemon juice*
*grated rind of ½ lemon*

**CAKE MIXTURE**
*6 oz (175g) self-raising flour*
*¼ teaspoon baking powder*
*½ teaspoon baking soda*
*¼ teaspoon salt*
*1 teaspoon cinnamon*
*¼ teaspoon ground nutmeg*
*¼ teaspoon ground cloves*
*2 oz (50g) butter*
*2 oz (50g) margarine*
*4 oz (100g) granulated sugar*
*2 oz (50g) brown sugar*
*2 large eggs*
*¼ pint (150ml) yoghurt*
*½ teaspoon vanilla essence*
*½ teaspoon almond essence*
*⅛ teaspoon lemon essence (optional)*
*⅛ teaspoon orange essence (optional)*

**1** Mix the first ten ingredients together and leave to stand overnight.

**2** When ready to make the cake preheat oven to 300°F (150°C, gas 2) and grease a 9 in (23cm) round cake tin. Flour the base of the tin only.

**3** Sift together the flour, baking powder, baking soda, salt, cinnamon, nutmeg and cloves, and set aside.

**4** Cream together the butter and margarine until soft and then beat in the sugar (brown and white).

**5** Blend in the eggs, yoghurt and essences.

**6** Add small amounts of the fruit mixture and flour mixture alternately to the creamed mixture and beat them in.

**7** When all the ingredients are well blended, spoon the mixture into the greased baking tin, level off with a knife and place in the oven.

**8** Bake for 1½ to 2 hours, until the blade of a knife inserted into the centre comes out clean.

**9** Turn the cake out to cool and then wrap it in foil. It tastes better if left to mature for a few days.

## YAOURTOPITA
### *Yoghurt cake*

A light, moist cake from Greece.

*6 oz (175g) butter*
*8 oz (250g) sugar*
*1 teaspoon grated lemon rind*
*4 eggs, separated*
*10 oz (300g) plain flour*
*1 teaspoon baking powder*
*1 teaspoon bicarbonate of soda*
*¼ teaspoon salt*
*4 fl oz (120ml) yoghurt*
*icing sugar for garnish*

**1** Put the butter, sugar and lemon rind in a large mixing bowl and beat until light and fluffy.

**2** Add the egg yolks and beat well.

**3** Sift the flour, baking powder, bicarbonate of soda and salt together.

**4** Add dry ingredients and yoghurt alternately to the mixture.

**5** Whisk egg whites until stiff and fold gently into the cake mixture.

**6** Pour quickly into a greased and floured 7½–8 in (18–20cm) round cake tin.

**7** Bake in an oven preheated to 350°F (180°C, gas 4) for about 1 hour or until the cake has shrunk away from the sides of the tin and is springy to the touch.

**8** Turn on to a wire rack and cool.

**9** Dust with icing sugar before serving.

## YOGHURT TATLISI

A light sponge soaked in syrup. Another recipe from Ifan Orga's *Cooking with Yogurt*. It is an adaptation of a well-known Turkish dessert. As this is rather a rich cake I suggest that you serve it as a tea-time treat.

*8 fl oz (250ml) yoghurt*
*12 oz (350g) icing sugar*
*2 tablespoons melted butter*
*4 eggs, separated*
*10 oz (300g) self-raising flour*
*½ teaspoon bicarbonate of soda*

GARNISH
*whipped cream*
*pralined whole almonds – brown*
    *whole almonds evenly in the oven*
    *sprinkling them frequently with*
    *icing sugar. The heat of the oven*
    *caramelizes the sugar*

SYRUP
*1 lb (450g) castor sugar*
*½ tablespoon lemon juice*

1  Pour the yoghurt into a mixing bowl and beat until creamy; stir in the icing sugar and butter.

2  Beat the egg yolks until thick and stir into the yoghurt mixture.

3  Sift the flour and soda together and fold into the batter.

4  Whisk the egg whites until stiff and fold gently into the sponge mixture.

5  Spoon into a greased and floured 8 in (20cm) cake tin, put into an oven preheated to 350°F (180°C, gas 4) and bake for about 1 hour.

6  Meanwhile make the syrup by boiling together the sugar, 1 pint (600ml) water and the lemon juice.

7  Simmer for 7 to 10 minutes and remove from the heat.

8  When the sponge is cooked remove it from the oven and pour the boiling syrup very slowly over it. (At this point keep the sponge in its tin.)

9  Leave to rest for about an hour by which time all the syrup should have been absorbed.

10  Cut into small pieces and serve on individual plates topped with whipped cream and the pralined almonds.

# GLOSSARY

**Besan**  Chick-pea flour. Used extensively in Indian cuisine; available from most stores selling Asian food.

**Black cumin seeds** (*Nigella sativa*)  Known as *kala zeera* in India. This is not a true cumin; it has a different, more aromatic and peppery flavour.

**Black mustard seeds** (*Brassica nigra*)  This variety is smaller and more pungent than the yellow variety; it is used in Indian, Middle Eastern and Gulf regional cooking.

**Burghul**  Hulled wheat, steamed until partly cooked, dried and then ground. It is available in 'fine' or 'coarse' grades – recipes specify which to use. Available in most Middle Eastern and Indian shops.

**Coriander leaves** (*Coriandrum sativum*)  A member of the parsley family. Both the leaves and seeds of this plant are used in the Middle East. It has a pungent flavour somewhat similar to dried orange peel.

**Feta**  Soft, crumbly white cheese made from goat's or ewe's milk. Available in most Middle Eastern shops.

**Garam masala**  A spice mixture containing black pepper, cardamom, cinnamon, cloves, nutmeg, black cumin, coriander and bay leaf. Can be purchased ready mixed from many shops.

**Ghee**  Pure butterfat. Ghee can be heated to a high temperature without burning. It is superior to ordinary butter and has a fragrance of its own. Used extensively in Indian and Middle Eastern cooking. Available in all Indian and Middle Eastern shops. *Samna* in Arabic.

**Haloumi**  A salty sheep's milk cheese, which is matured in whey. Sometimes flavoured with mint or black cumin.

**Kaymak** or **Ser**  A thick cream which can literally be cut with a knife; usually prepared with buffalo's milk. The nearest substitute is thick clotted cream.

197

**Kewra**   A variety of screwpine (*Pandanus odoratissimus*). Mostly used for flavouring Indian sweets. Can be bought as an essence or concentrate. It is strong and one drop is usually enough.

**Polenta**   Maize (corn) flour dried in the open, not in the oven. Can be purchased from Italian and Balkan food stores and from health shops.

**Sumak** (*Rhus corioria*)   The dried, crushed red berries of a species of the sumach tree. It has a sour, lemony taste. Crush and steep it in water to extract its essence, which can then be used in stews instead of lemon juice.

**Tahina**   A nutty flavoured oily paste made from toasted sesame seeds. If left standing it tends to separate and needs to be blended before use. Available in all Middle Eastern stores.

**Tourshi**   Pickles, a must on any Middle Eastern dinner table. Small cucumbers, chilli peppers, carrots, aubergines, cauliflowers, etc., are home pickled and often served as the only accompaniment to a meat dish.

# INDEX